The Power of Persuasion

Harry Hazel

Sheed & Ward

Sheed & Ward™ is a service of National Catholic Reporter Publishing
Company, Inc.

Library of Congress Catalog Card Number: 88-61856

ISBN: 1-55612-211-X

Published by: Sheed & Ward
115 E. Armour Blvd., P.O. Box 419492
Kansas City, MO 64141-6492

To order, call: (800) 333-7373

Contents

Dedication

Dedicated to Dominic LaRusso, master teacher, persuader and friend.

Acknowledgements

I want to thank a number of colleagues who helped me on this book. Michael Herzog, Anita Foreman and Charlene Dupper read the first draft. All three gave me encouragement and the feedback I needed to make the pages more readable. Sally Clark and Lori Zimmerman took time out of their busy schedules to proofread later drafts. I thank them for that and their words of good cheer.

Preface

"A sharp, two-edged sword came out of his mouth, and his face shone like the sun at its brightest." —*Revelation* 1:16

If baseball, Chevrolets and apple pie are American, so is persuasion. Virtually no other country has as many politicians, salespeople, advertisers, attorneys and religious preachers who practice this art form on such a regular basis. The North American economy is fueled by the fires of motivation. Consumers often buy products they don't need because someone has convinced them they do. Americans continue to influence and be influenced by each other as they sell everything from soap to skyscrapers.

Persuasion cuts two ways: it can help or hurt. It helps us get jobs, earn a living and has a profound impact on those people who are important to us. But it can cost us more money than we can afford to spend and get us tangled in commitments we don't want to make.

All of us are involved in persuasion on a daily basis. Some are already proficient at persuading and make a living at it. Others are vulnerable to any new scam that comes along. Few of us are so consistently hard-headed that we always make decisions based on reason and forethought. Many of us are not even aware of the tactics we use or are used on us. Persuasion is a tool we can use to help us advance our careers and present ideas we believe are important. But it's also a process that can get us into debt, make decisions we wish we hadn't made and cause us grief because we should have known better than to fall for some fast-talking huckster.

Treatises on persuasion have been around since at least the fifth century B.C. with titles ranging from Aristotle's *Rhetoric* to Robert Conklin's *How to Get People to Do Things*. Numerous texts have been available and I've used a number of them myself because I've taught Persuasion as a college class for the past seventeen years. I've also conducted workshops for professionals on topics like improving sales techniques and motivating others. College texts contain a wealth of information and research on persuasion but, for the most part, lean toward the theoretical and are written in an "academic style." In this book, I've taken some basic principles of motivation and tried to explain them with the method I use when I teach the subject.

Most people can sharpen a skill by following three steps: (1) look at models of proven practitioners, (2) study the methods they used and then (3) apply them. In my experience as a teacher, I've noticed that students seem to learn best when they start with concrete, intriguing people who are or were really good at influencing. The next step is to examine *why* their approach worked so well—or failed. This stage involves looking at the theories of persuasion to see if they match what practitioners really do when they try to influence others. The final stage is to take the lessons learned from others and relate them to ourselves.

While virtually everyone persuades, very few standout as eloquent practitioners of the art. Highly successful motivators like John Kennedy, Martin Luther King and Winston Churchill are relatively rare. But none of these three leaders came by their persuasive ability naturally. They worked hard to master a skill they considered important to their career, cause and country. Most of us can learn to be better motivators ourselves by studying their techniques.

In this book, I present practical techniques of persuasion and concentrate on motivators who excelled. Such people range from the pope who launched the Crusades with a speech historians have called the most influential in history to a Spokane prosecuting attorney who helped convict a highly-publicized rapist. Sometimes I use examples of effective persuaders who have failed, because they, too, can teach valuable lessons about what works and what doesn't.

The people in these pages are motivators who got results. Some of them, like Mother Teresa and Martin Luther King, have used their influence to help their sisters and brothers. Others, like Jim Jones, have weaved their motivational magic to get followers to kill. But they all have one trait in common—they knew how to move an audience.

Because persuasion is a double-edged sword, the book takes two major directions. The first part includes an examination of successful persuaders to see how they worked and what made them succeed. The second section focuses on ways to protect ourselves from being manipulated. We may have a hard time saying no to a persuasive pitch when we should because the person asking us is such an adept motivator. Sometimes, our children or friends join cults because they've been mesmerized by an eloquent recruiter. Or perhaps we've been conned into voting for a politician who knows how to work a crowd but isn't a strong advocate of issues that we believe are important in improving human lives.

Most of us can benefit by knowing more about persuasion. We have to constantly sell ourselves and our ideas if we want to find the right job, get married, convince family members or promote an idea. We can also protect ourselves from becoming prey to unwanted products or harmful ideas. In the process, we can save money and prevent ourselves from doing something we'll later regret. In short, we'll learn more about a force that plays such a dominant role in our lives.

1

The Secret of the Effective Persuader

Some have called it the most effective speech in recorded history.[1] On November 25, 1095, Pope Urban II convinced his audience to go east and rescue the Holy Land from the Seljuk Turks. Most historians agree that the oration was the catalyst that set the Crusades in motion.

Urban II was surprised by the astounding success of his speech. So powerful was the talk that the crowd of 5,000 stood up and in unison shouted "God wills it." Knights, bishops and noblemen scrambled to make preparations for the first of five Crusades which were waged over the next two centuries. Urban galvanized some of his listeners into immediate action. A disorganized band of pilgrims traveled to Constantinople where they were told by Emperor Alexius Comnenus to go home. Convinced that Urban's message was divinely inspired, the pilgrims plunged ahead anyway and made an attack on the Turks, who promptly annihilated them. Months later, the more disciplined armies of France and Normandy arrived in the East and took on the Turks in what turned out to be the most successful of the Five Crusades.

It's a shame that such a powerful speech was used to motivate men to take up arms, even though the participants considered their cause just and even noble. Ideally, the most effective speech in history might have been directed toward helping the hungry, serving the poor or urging people to develop their talents. But the oration provides some important insights about why persuasion works well and how a skilled motivator like Urban

1

could propel his audience into a movement that would have such a profound impact on history.

What kind of power was Urban able to exert on his audience? Why did he succeed when other popes before him had failed? And why does his performance illustrate the "secret" of successful persuasion? The occasion can be a historic speech, a sales pitch or a sermon, but the "secret" is the same.

Urban's predecessor, Gregory VII, had tried to launch a massive military effort some twenty years before. In 1073, the Byzantine Emperor, Michael VII, had asked Gregory for help against the Turks after the Seljuk armies won a devastating victory at Manzikert. As a result, the Turks held most of Asia Minor. Gregory issued an encyclical on the matter and proclaimed that he was personally ready to lead the crusading armies eastward. But the pope became sidetracked in a prolonged dispute with the German King Henry IV and was not able to launch his plans.

In 1088, a French nobleman named Odo de Lagery was elected pope and took the name, Urban II. This new pontiff was different from his predecessor Gregory, primarily in his persuasive methods. While Gregory was stern and arrogant, Urban was polished and diplomatic. Gregory ordered and Urban persuaded. Within seven years, he had weaved his spell so effectively that he was the spiritual master of western Christendom by the time he called the Council of Clermont in 1095.

The pope invited both bishops and noblemen to attend the Council in Southern France. Urban's announced purpose was to reinforce the "Truce of God," a directive forbidding Christians to spill the blood of a fellow Christian. Such a truce had been largely ignored by many young noblemen who were brought up in a culture that encouraged knights to demonstrate their manhood by fighting. Military prowess was also a quick way to gain land from one's weaker neighbors. As a result, Europe was losing many of its young men as they killed each other for land and pride.

Persuasion takes place when a motivator is able to either change or confirm an existing attitude in the minds of listeners. An attitude can't be taken out of the head and examined under a microscope. Attitudes are hard to read in a listener and this helps explain why persuasion is such a challenging art. Good persuaders are especially skilled in analyzing the attitudes of their audience and then adapting their messages to what they've found. To ignore this principle is to miss one of the most important ingredients in motivation.

Successful persuaders like Urban II *begin* by establishing specific goals and then examining the attitudes of their audience. They don't present their message first. Many a sales attempt has gone awry because the salesperson tried to push his message without first analyzing customer attitudes. The stereotype of the fast-talking hustler in the lime green leisure suit has been well established. He comes up to the customer, flashes a smile, introduces himself and then spouts three reasons for buying his product. Experienced pros, on the other hand, make sure they know exactly the belief system, values and attitudes of their customers before they start delivering their message. This is the secret of their success. Examine any proven motivator and the pattern is clear—persuasion is powerful when strategy is matched to a discovery of the wants and needs of an audience.

Urban's Strategy

Urban's perceptive assessment of his audience was the key to his success. He read his listeners well. He knew the crusading ideal which was floating in the air, thanks to the efforts of his predecessor, Gregory VII. He also recognized that the young knights in the audience were conditioned by a spirit of chivalry. A study of the songs, poetry and writings of the era show a strong psychology of fighting battles to gain honor, a lady fair and material treasures. One popular poem in particular influenced the knights. The *Song of Roland* was a lengthy narrative piece which glorified Charlemagne and his soldiers as fearless Christian warriors riding off to do battle with the hated heathens.

The pope was shrewd enough to recognize that many of the knights were not regular church-goers, but that they still feared God's wrath for their sins. The Church had continually reminded them that killing a fellow

Christian was in direct violation of the "Truce of God" and that anyone who died after committing this most grievous mortal sin would go to hell. While the urge to follow the medieval code of fighting to demonstrate manhood was stronger than the need to avoid committing a mortal sin, thoughts of damnation lingered in the outer edges of the knights' consciousness. Urban correctly concluded that the nobles were torn between two contrasting drives.

Urban also knew that there were other less important, but influential attitudes in his hearers. Most Christians were embarrassed that Jerusalem, the site of Christ's death and resurrection, had for centuries been in the hands of the despised heathens. This prevented Christian pilgrims ready access to the Holy City and made them easy prey to the constant attacks by robbers who roamed the roads leading to the Holy Land.

Based on his careful audience analysis, Urban presented five themes in his talk: (1) the necessity of helping suffering Christians in the East, (2) the threat of the Turks, (3) the desecration of holy shrines in Jerusalem, (4) the need to re-channel hostile feelings against fellow Christians to the heathens, and (5) an emphasis that the Crusade would be God's work.

Urban's arrangement of themes was crucial in producing the persuasive effect he wanted. Like an eloquent and fiery football coach rallying his team before the big game, the pope started with some emotional references to injuries suffered by Christian pilgrims who were trying to visit the shrines. Most Europeans had heard about the atrocities, but Urban graphically described how the pilgrims were being attacked and killed. For the military-minded knights, this situation was an intolerable affront to their pride.

The speaker then concentrated on the imminent threat of the Turks to western Europe. He stressed that the Seljuks were poised to attack Constantinople. He went on to emphasize that the Turks had already conquered a number of countries with the efficiency of a sickle cutting wheat. Not only were Christians killed in the battles, but survivors were led off to slavery. The pontiff described the Turks as "a race so despised, so degenerate and slave of the demons."[2] He went on to brand his foes as agents of Satan who fully intended to attack Europe after they had disposed of Constantinople. Urban described the "domino argument" that would become a standard strategy for leaders who wanted to rally a nation to war.

To reinforce the demonic qualities of the heathens, the pope used some of his most graphic language in describing the desecration of the holy shrines in Jerusalem—places which held such a special reverence for Christians. He asked his audience members to imagine animal blood being poured on the tombs of Christ and His Mother. If that were not enough to enrage his listeners, he went on to remind them that these same shrines now housed pagan idols.

The pope's first three arguments enkindled wrath, but they were presented as the foundations of his two most effective themes: the need to re-direct hostile feelings toward the heathens to avoid personal damnation and the conviction that a crusade would be God's work.

Despite some variations of wording, the chroniclers who recorded the speech emphasize that the re-directing of hostile tendencies toward the Turks was the key argument in the oration. The pope vividly reminded knights and warriors that the Truce of God had been continually violated and that such a sin not only decimated Europe's male population, but placed the murderer in direct threat of eternal damnation. To die without confession after such a heinous crime was to be doomed to everlasting punishment.

In effect, Urban was providing a legitimate outlet for the hostile urges which dominated a soldier's life. No longer would the knights have to bear the burden of guilt for killing a fellow Christian. They could re-direct their bellicose feelings toward an avowed and despised enemy. The pope solved a basic dilemma for his listeners. On the one hand, the soldiers were taught that fighting was good because it helped prove manhood and gain land. But killing also had a down-side because it was a mortal sin. God's representative on earth, the embodiment of Christ Himself, told his audience that fighting was praiseworthy if done for a good cause. What cause could be more noble than rescuing the Holy Land from the heathens and in the bargain protecting Western Europe from the threat of the Seljuks?

As final reinforcement, Urban proclaimed that participants could gain both eternal and temporal rewards. The pope reminded the soldiers that they would be honored through the ages if they marched eastward. Centuries later, they would be remembered as the heroes who freed the Holy Land. As an added benefit, the pope offered the tantalizing prospect of material treasures which could be gained by the adventure.

In his conclusion, Urban stressed that this noble call was being issued by Christ Himself and that the pope was merely an instrument of delivery. As Christ's representative on earth, Urban promised a plenary indulgence to all who were killed in the Crusade. No matter what their fate, the participants couldn't lose. If they survived, they could gain material bounty and be part of the most noble cause on earth. If they died, they would receive everlasting glory on earth and have a direct ticket to heaven.

Application

While most Christians would have a hard time reconciling some of the pope's ideas with Christ's message of love and turning the other cheek, the oration helps explain why highly effective persuasive efforts succeed and others fail. The Urban speech is presented here not to justify its message, but to demonstrate how a strong persuader works. The speech is a historic and dramatic example of successful motivation, but the same tactics used by the pope can be found in any highly effective motivational message.

Earlier, I stated that successful persuaders begin by clearly defining their motivational goal. Then, they carefully analyze their audience to discover their beliefs, values and group norms. They don't present their message until these key steps have been taken. Urban was well aware that members of his audience were part of a culture which extolled fighting. But at the same time, the soldiers carried a burden of guilt if they killed fellow Christians. Thus, they were torn between adherence to a dominant 12th century cultural norm and a moral standard which forbade fighting.

The pope addressed both problems by blending strong needs for security, honor, hostility and the alleviation of guilt into one integrated image. What had been garbled and troublesome in the minds of his audience now became clear. Such a bonded image became the catalyst for action.

Urban's oration contains a number of lessons for anyone who wants to improve the art of influencing. Instead of starting a historical movement, we may need to do well interviewing for a job, selling a product, courting a potential marriage partner or convincing family members to go along with an idea.

Take, for example, the job interview. It seems ironic that a woman or man can go through four years of college, spend around $40,000 in the process and know that getting the right job depends on how well she or he communicates in an interview. Evidence suggests that employers hire not so much on the basis of how prospects can perform a particular set of skills once they're hired, but how they perform during the interview.

When I was in graduate school, there was a fellow student who had mastered the art of the job interview. (Let's call him Frank.) Normally, Frank wore tattered jeans, a scruffy T-shirt and an army jacket from World War II. He also sported the typical early seventies grad school look—a beard and shoulder length hair. But every spring, he would get bored with the routine of his studies and the smallness of the town which skirted the university. His escape was to apply for teaching jobs, even though he knew he couldn't accept any positions that year since he hadn't finished his studies. Frank simply wanted some diversion and a way to get out of town.

After doing his homework on a particular school, he sent out his carefully worded letters of application. His letters were a delicate blend of sincere interest, knowledge of the job and familiarity with the institution. When he landed an interview—and he usually got at least two per year— he made his biannual visit to the barber for his "job interview" haircut. For the interview, Frank would exchange his grad school uniform for a dark blue suit, conservative red tie and starched white shirt. If clothing expert

John Molloy had been writing in those days, he might have used the transformed Frank as a model.

Days before the interview, Frank read the institution's catalog, called his friends who worked there to find out about the interviewers and their prevailing beliefs. He then imagined the scene and rehearsed his role. After flying in for the interview, he was a model of the successful job applicant—well-groomed, sincere, and in complete command of himself. He presented a well balanced combination of questions and comments. He listened attentively to the interviewers' questions and answered them precisely without going into rambling detail. At all times, he was affable and straight-forward. As a result, the search chairperson often offered Frank the job which he had to politely turn down a week later because, regrettably, he needed to finish graduate school. He was sorry about the expense incurred for plane ticket, lodging and meals. Perhaps, when he finished his studies, he would re-apply for a job at the same college. Sure.

What do an 11th century pope and a bored, glib graduate student have in common? They were both successful persuaders who followed the same steps. Each had a specific goal. Each analyzed his audience carefully with a particular emphasis on discovering the attitudes of his listeners. Both took time to find the prevailing belief systems of their persuasive targets. Each shaped his message according to what he learned.

Reconciling Two Clashing Perspectives

Part of Urban's success stems from his ability to bring together two ideas that seemed contradictory before the speech. The knights saw no way to reconcile their urge to fight with doing God's will. Urban pulled the two ideas together in an integrated image—the same tactic often used by successful salespeople. For example, suppose a customer really likes a new car but can't see how the payments will fit into the family budget. He emphatically tells the salesperson that there is no way he can go beyond payments of $225 per month. The cost of his dream car would stretch a 48-month contract to $350 a month—obviously way over a tight family budget. Does the effective salesperson get flustered or discouraged? No, she empathizes with the customer's dilemma and then offers two options. Either the man can stretch the installment loan to 60 months and have the payments come to around $275 a month, or he can lease the car and get monthly payments close to the desired amount.

What if the customer is leery of leasing since he's never followed this approach before? He has always taken great pride in *owning* his cars. For him, leasing means the credit agency owns this mobile extension of himself. Sensing this conflict by asking questions, listening carefully and picking up non-verbal cues, the salesperson asks how often the customer trades in the family car. Learning that the man likes to get a new car every three or four years, she deftly points out that leasing might just be the perfect plan. She mentions that payments will be relatively low—at least close to his predetermined budget—and that for someone who changes cars as often as he does, the lease plan would probably be best. Sure, she says, if you held onto a car for seven to ten years, it would be better to buy. In the conversation, she discovers that the customer grew up in California, so she quietly mentions that almost 75 percent of cars in California are now leased and it will only be a matter of time and good judgment before the rest of the country follows this trend-setter. Besides, this new model is one of the safest on the highway so you'll be doing your family a big favor as well as getting what you really want. That's the clincher as salesperson and customer walk to her office to "finish the paperwork." The happy customer drives off in the gleaming new car, feeling excited and relieved of the guilt which might have been imposed by going over budget. And the salesperson has another commission.

While the situation of Urban talking to the knights is vastly different from the salesperson putting the finishing touches on her sale, both have applied the same motivational device. They've taken two disparate ideas and fused them into one. Whether the guilt is over killing fellow Christians or cutting into the family budget, the *feeling* is the same. Relieve the burden of mental dissonance, and the way is clear to move people further down the road to action.[3]

The Key to Persuasion

Robert Conklin provides one of the main keys to successful persuasion: "To the degree you give others what they want, they will give you what you want."[4] Too often, people are so consumed with the correctness of an idea that they're convinced that someone else has to see it the same way. While it's true that enthusiasm for a cause is important, the message has to be one the audience is open to accepting. If a parent wants to convince a family member that buckling up in the car saves lives and prevents injuries, he might conclude that no one can argue with this basic premise. Armed with such a conviction, he plods on with little chance of success. If the family member is not open to such an idea at the moment, the most eloquent persuasive message in the world won't work and the passenger continues to ride unbuckled.

People respond to appeals that satisfy their strongest needs. Such needs are based on what they believe is important to them. What *they* believe shapes their attitudes. Therefore the expert persuader asks a series of questions: what do these folks really believe? What is important to them—not to me? How does their primary group—family, school, work institutions—see the world? Armed with this information, the expert then sculpts arguments around the attitudes he's discovered in his audience.

The Importance of Attitudes

An attitude is a predisposition to respond positively or negatively to a persuasive message.[5] Unlike opinions which are easy to change, attitudes have usually become deeply ingrained in the psyche of each person over a long period. Our attitudes about abortion, capital punishment, women's rights or religion are not passing fancies which change on a daily basis. They've been built up over a number of years, usually as a result of messages we've heard from parents, teachers and others who have influenced us.

Our attitudes are anchored by our belief system and what we value.[6] If I believe in God, I might value keeping in touch through prayer and going to church. If I don't believe, it's not important for me to pray or attend services on Sunday. If we're firmly convinced that the arms race is getting completely out of control, we might very well carry signs outside a nuclear power plant. If we occasionally worry about it but conclude that whatever will be, will be, we'll tend to distract ourselves and banish the thought to the outer fringes of our mind.

We're also conditioned by the group we belong to. Numerous studies have documented the power of groups in shaping individual attitudes. If we join the Marines, a fraternity, or a garden club, we're influenced by the customs of our group. It takes gumption to go against the established norms of a group. The deviant is quickly ostracized and usually quits the group or conforms to their standards. This strong pull of the group helps explain the conformity and sameness of the individual members. Shriners dress in the same kind of outfits. So do Marines and members of religious groups. Studies show that requiring grade and high school students to wear uniforms conditions them to conform to school standards and rules.

There's a principle in sales that customers don't buy a product as much as they buy the *benefits* they believe the product will bring. Exercise enthusiasts don't purchase the sweat and hard work but the image of themselves as toned up and looking good—or at least better than they did before they signed up for the program. The motivator who focuses on the features or advantages of the idea or product is halfway home. Urban did precisely that when he reminded the Knights that not only would they have an honorable outlet for their fighting but they would gain the double benefit of earthly and eternal gains. They might find land in the unknown but tantalizing east. And if they died in battle, they would be remembered as heroes and gain eternal salvation. If Urban had simply commanded them to stop fighting with their fellow Christians, such an appeal would have fallen on deaf ears as it had so many times before. But by highlighting the benefits, this pope succeeded where others failed. The salesperson used the same strategy when she pointed out the twin advantages of leasing—having the car of choice at affordable monthly payments.

Overcoming Objections

If we're not persuaded after the motivator has spent some time with us, it's because some major or minor objection is hovering in our mind. We may like the new suit of clothes, but we don't like the price tag attached. We might want to take a college evening course, but we don't relish the thought of breaking away from our family for three hours on Tuesday and Thursday nights. An effective motivator looks for the major obstacle to persuasion and then tries to deal with it. She doesn't avoid it because she realizes that by doing so, she won't persuade. Urban was well aware that the knights were reluctant to give up their fighting. It wasn't enough to ask for a cease-fire among Christian soldiers. This had been tried many times before with the Peace of God, but such directives had been largely ignored. But when the Pope turned the obstacle into an advantage, he broke through the motivational barriers that had stopped so many of his papal predecessors.

I knew a college student who used the same tactic with her parents. They didn't want her to take a weekend ski trip with her friends because they thought she was behind in her studies. So two weeks before the trip, she called her parents and presented the following line of argument: "Mom and Dad, I realize that you believe my studies are very important and I completely agree. I also know that you fear I'll lose some valuable study time if I take the trip to Red Mountain in two weeks. Therefore, I want to make a promise. I'll put in extra hours till trip time and that time will equal what I would have spent had I stayed here in the dorm demoralized and bored. In addition, the break from my studies will give me a new vigor as I face the books Monday morning. I'll *want* to go back to my studies." Sound like a line? It worked.

Summary of Key Points

1. Successful motivators like Pope Urban II begin by clearly defining specific goals they want to accomplish. They then look for ways to reach those goals.

2. The "secret" of persuasion is a careful analysis of an audience's wants, attitudes, values, beliefs and group norms. The best persuaders put aside their own convictions and examine the listener's point of view. Then they shape their message around what they've found.

3. Strong motivators are especially good at reconciling what appear to be two contradictory images in the minds of their hearers. Effective persuaders clear up the confusion existing in the mind of the audience and reduce their feelings of discomfort. Such motivators help listeners see a message in a new way that will help them fulfill their strongest needs or wants.

4. Persuasion works best when a speaker promotes the *benefits* of an idea or product. People respond more to what they perceive as advantages or features rather than the product or idea itself.

5. Effective motivators look for and try to draw out any objections that would prevent listeners from buying their message. Rather than trying to discount such objections, they empathize with their hearers and then try to show how what appears to be an objection can be turned to an advantage.

2

The Power of
Personal Appeal

A stranger walks up to us at a crowded meeting, flashes a smile, grabs our hand and tells us she's really glad to meet us. She asks where we're from and then listens intently as we tell her. She asks us how we like the conference and then nods in agreement as we tell her that some talks are good and others are a waste of time. We like her and really don't mind too much when she asks us to help serve on next year's awards nomination committee.

Robert Cialdini calls this liking the "friendly thief"[1] because, if we like someone we're much more open to their influence. It's hard to say no to a salesman who has become a friend—even if the friendship was developed over the half hour it took to sell the car. It's far easier to turn down a persuader we don't like. So what makes one person more appealing than another?

Despite a common misconception, liking is not necessarily linked to physical attractiveness. While the beautiful woman or handsome man might have an edge in motivating, most of us know good-looking people who are *unlikable*. We initially make a judgement about someone's attractiveness during the first few seconds of meeting her, but that first impression rises or falls depending on other factors. If the good-looking person is also friendly, we tend to like her even more. But if she's cold, aloof and arrogant, her attractiveness takes a quick nosedive.

On the other hand, we might meet someone who doesn't fit into the same category as a Tom Selleck or Brooke Shields. We may even perceive the person as plain or below average. But the look in her eye and the warmth in her face is magnetic. As attractiveness increases, so does the ability to persuade.

Ethos

In his treatise on persuasion, Aristotle calls personal appeal "ethos." Ethos is the image of integrity and goodwill a speaker projects to an audience.[2]

Contemporary experts on the subject of ethos—or source credibility— list a number of persuasive qualities, but four have emerged from Aristotle's original description: perceived competence, the impression of integrity, rapport, and identification with persuadees. Ethos is how people *perceive* a persuader and not necessarily what he really is. A salesperson, preacher or politician may *appear* to be capable and honest, but could be doing a clever job of hiding his shallowness and deceit. On the other hand, someone might seem to be a mental lightweight and a charlatan, but could be highly intelligent and totally honest. Perhaps a halting speech pattern and a devious-looking goatee[3] convey this image. An audience often gets what it sees but not always. Often what an audience sees shapes how it will be influenced.

Cultivating Ethos Takes Time and Training

Most successful motivators have worked hard to hone their personal appeal, even though they make it look natural and easy. The Latin adage *Ars est celare artem* (art is to hide art) applies to most top persuaders. Just as some athletes make their performance appear effortless, so do speakers who are really good at motivating others.

No one gave John Kennedy much chance of winning in 1960. His opponent in the first televised presidential debate was the experienced orator Richard Nixon. But when Kennedy stepped before the cameras on September 26, 1960, he looked poised and he spoke with the polished exuberance of a man who had prepared thoroughly. His crisp New England accent, suntanned face and well-tailored figure were as important in the outcome as the arguments he used in that hour of verbal jousting with his adversary. Democrats were delighted at the unexpected eloquence of their young candidate. Some Republicans, on the other hand, thought their front-runner had been sabotaged by heavy make-up and a grey suit which made the Vice President seem to fade into an equally grey background. His apparent nervousness didn't help since Nixon was supposed to be the calm and assured gladiator who would easily win the battle of words and ideas. The first Kennedy-Nixon debate was pivotal in convincing many viewers to vote for the young senator from Massachusetts.

Anyone who carefully reads the written transcript of the first debate would have to conclude that Nixon was the winner on logical points. He supported his claims with more evidence and did a better job of counteracting his opponent's arguments. But for the majority of viewers, Kennedy's *image* or ethos was the deciding factor. He projected a controlled dynamism that made many voters conclude that he would be a strong leader and effective president.

Kennedy worked hard to improve his ethos. Before the debates, he wasn't considered a particularly eloquent orator. Experts judged Nixon a more polished and experienced debater. But Kennedy was determined to improve. He worked with a speech instructor during the 1960 campaign to help him get rid of some rough edges and fine-tune his delivery. He had spoken too rapidly and didn't pause in the right places. Some listeners found his Boston accent and short, choppy gestures distracting. Kennedy improved his public speaking skills because he knew how important they were in harvesting votes.

Kennedy visited Gonzaga University in February, 1960, when I was a student there and I vividly remember the impact he made on his listeners. At the time, he was not even the front-runner for the Democratic Party. As he walked on the stage of the venerable old Gonzaga gymnasium, the audience knew Kennedy was someone special. He projected an air of confidence and understated elegance as he started to speak. His animation increased as he punctured the air with short, staccato-like gestures. Afterwards, he fielded questions with the easy grace of a politician who had heard it all before.

When Kennedy left the gym and walked toward Crosby Library, a crowd quickly surrounded him and made it clear they wanted more. Repeatedly, he stopped to spray his smile at the on-lookers and patiently answer their questions.

Personal Appeal and Perceived Competence

Kennedy's performance, especially in the first presidential debate, highlights the importance of perceived competence for a speaker. An audience is far more inclined to be persuaded by someone they believe is highly capable, confident and an expert on the subject. Knowing he was behind in the polls, Kennedy and his advisors, Ted Sorenson, Richard Goodwin and Mike Feldman, studied like driven grad students in the days before the debate. The three grilled their candidate with questions and didn't let him rest until he could answer with the poised and energetic assurance which became his hallmark.[4]

Kennedy appeared to have more command of facts and figures than his adversary. Kennedy's voice also sounded more relaxed and confident. The usually eloquent Nixon came across as hesitant in some of his answers.

An effective motivator telegraphs the non-verbal message that he knows what he's talking about. If a speaker seems uncertain of his material, his persuasive power quickly erodes. He can wear a $700 wool suit, have a rich, baritone voice and the best visual aids in town, but if he doesn't project an image of confident preparation, he'll have a hard time convincing an audience.

Listeners are far more inclined to listen to a speaker they consider an expert on a topic. Three speakers can give the same talk with widely different results. A financial planner with thirty years experience, a freshman in high school, and a reformed gambler could all deliver exactly the same five minute speech entitled "How to get maximum mileage from your investments during the hard times," and the impact would vary dramatically. The gambler might have the best delivery, but most people would think twice before accepting his message, even though it was identical to that of the financial planner.

The Aura of Integrity

When Aristotle discusses ethos in his *Rhetoric*, he links it directly to the moral quality a speaker projects to an audience. He also underscores the image of integrity as the most important factor in persuasion.[5] Take away a motivator's moral character in the minds of the audience, and his power evaporates. During the early stages of the 1988 Presidential race, Gary Hart's campaign was dismantled on the one issue of perceived integrity. Despite Hart's protestations that his personal life should not be linked to his ability to be an effective president, the vast majority of voters didn't buy that argument and consequently Hart wisely chose to withdraw early. When he re-entered the race in December of 1987, Hart declared, "Let the people decide." They did. Even though a few faithful followers were delighted with his decision, the majority found his perceived character flaw too big a hurdle to let him get very far down the road to the presidency.

Some have pointed out that Hart was not much different from John Kennedy in his fondness for women other than his wife. But, of course, the essential difference is that voters were not *aware* of the rumors about Kennedy. If they were, Kennedy would have had little chance of winning, especially since his 1960 race with Nixon was so close. If the public had perceived a morally tarnished Kennedy, his candidacy would have crumbled. Conversely, most voters stopped focusing on front-runner Hart's strengths as they watched the scandal unfold in the media. Take away the foundation of a persuader's moral character, and often the rest of the house falls.

Integrity can be the strongest facet of a persuader's ethos. In 1980, Mother Teresa spoke to a crowd of students at Harvard: "I am told that some of you are having premarital sex. And I hear that some of you even are getting abortions. I must tell you this is wrong."[6] Very few could come on this strong to a college audience without getting hooted out of the auditorium. But Mother Teresa's personal integrity and intense conviction gives her unusual persuasive power.

Clothes Help Make the Motivator

Kenneth Burke compares successful persuasion to a well produced play. Just as a theater production features actors, scenes, a plot and a script, so also does a successful persuasive event like a televised debate or press conference. Like actresses and actors, skilled motivators must wear the right costume because clothing is an important part of source credibility. We may feel overdosed on books about clothes and image, but the right outfit helps persuade. Since so many people function primarily in the visual zone, how a persuader looks and what she wears will often pack more punch than her ideas, no matter how logical or well-organized those ideas are.

Clothes expert John Molloy has described "the success uniform."[7] Men and women who want to influence are advised to wear a suit with a wool look. Polyester is out because it murmurs "cheap and tacky." The would-be executive is better off wearing Fidel Castro fatigues than clothes with the polyester look.

For both women and men, the image should be crisp, professional and attractive. This can be achieved with the well-tailored wool-blend business suit. Molloy advises women to avoid the "pants and tie" because such a combination makes a woman look too much like a man. The woman executive betrays herself by wearing an outfit that would be perfect for the evening social gathering, but would be out of place for the morning board meeting at IBM. Molloy advises a skirt, jacket and a blouse and feminine scarf to signal the right blend of strength and femininity.

In our society, women face a unique challenge in projecting ethos because they have to walk a fine line between assertiveness and femininity. If they come across as strong and abrasive, they're seen as too masculine. But if they're too soft and gentle, they don't project the aura of strength so vital for effective ethos. Clothing is one way to project the best image for a woman, and the way she dresses communicates a key message about femininity and strength.

Television journalists Jane Pauley, Diane Sawyer and Barbara Walters are good examples of women who blend vigor with femininity. Margaret Thatcher sends out the same message. All exude strength, but no one would call them masculine. Each dresses in a way that reflects professionalism. Their intelligence, command of language, and poise all contribute to a strong ethos, but the right clothes gives them an edge.

Attorneys, executives and salespeople are keenly aware of the power of clothing to create and maintain a positive impression. Lawyers wear suits to create a distinct impact in court, but they also make sure their clients are dressed to convey a look of innocence. The visual impact in a court trial is crucial because the accused sits for days without uttering a word. If he wore his normal attire or the outfit he was arrested in, his chances of acquittal would plummet. The scruffy army jacket, the "Born to kill" tattoo, the faded jeans torn at the knees, the scraggly beard and unkempt hair shout the message "I'm as guilty as I look." But spruce him up, put him in a conservative wool two piece suit, trim his hair and beard, and he comes across as someone who won last month's outstanding young businessman's award.

Research shows that the best outfit is one which reflects authority and is a slight cut above clothing worn by peers. The legendary Joe Girard dresses like the customers who buy the cars he sells. In *How to Sell Anything to Anybody*,[8] Girard says he loves to wear suits, but doesn't do so because he would appear too different from the blue collar customers who make up his clientele. He dresses in slacks and a shirt, but not any old pair of pants or shirt. His clothes send out the message that he's like his customers, but the clothes he buys are a cut above the rest. He appears as a super-representative of his kind of people.

John Kennedy's darker suit the night of the first televised debate should not have been a key ingredient in his better performance against Richard Nixon, but it was. The dark tones and well tailored look simply made him appear more polished than his grey suited opponent.

Besides the impression clothes telegraph to an audience, the right or wrong clothes also affect the persuader. If a speaker doesn't feel she has the right dress for the occasion, her confidence and fluency suffer. Standing before an audience, the speaker thinks "Why didn't I wear my best suit"? The focus shifts to an uncomfortable feeling of not being dressed properly for the topic and audience. The best motivators analyze the occasion, put on the appropriate outfit, forget about it, and concentrate on the subject and listeners.

Personal Appeal and the Voice

Most Americans who heard the voice of General Douglas MacArthur will never forget how he sounded. After a distinguished and turbulent military career, MacArthur said good-bye to the nation in 1951. His speech "Honor, Duty and Country" was eloquent and emotional. President Truman had dismissed him as supreme Allied Commander in the Far East after a power struggle which Commander-in-Chief Truman won. Most listeners vividly recall the final, ringing phrase, "Old soldiers never die, they just fade away." The haunting quality in MacArthur's voice made his words linger in the mind long after he spoke them.

Like MacArthur, skilled orators use their voice to touch the emotions of a crowd. The really good ones play it like a musical instrument in grabbing their listeners and keeping them riveted to the message. Most people don't really know how they sound and are unaware of how much their voice affects their ability to persuade. If we've heard our voice on a tape recorder within the last six months, we have a hard time believing that the sound is really ours. A typical comment is, "That isn't me, that's my brother." This reaction is understandable because we don't hear our own voices accurately. (Also, family members tend to have similar voices.) The sound leaves the larynx and travels on its muffled journey through the bones of our head. We also hear the voice indirectly as it bounces off walls and any other outside object and then makes its way back to our ears. Consequently, the sound is distorted.

A speaker with an unpleasant voice can create the same effect as a teacher running a fingernail down a blackboard. A manager can have well-reasoned arguments and be impeccably dressed, but if his voice is strident or whiny, his impact as a motivator drops. If the speaker's voice is controlled, poised and pleasant, an audience is much more likely to be influenced by what he says.

So What To Do?

If we've heard our voice recently and don't like the sound, there's hope if we're willing to take some steps to improve delivery. Dorothy Sarnoff has written a very practical book *Speech Can Change Your Life*[9] in which she emphasizes that the voice is one of the primary indicators of personality and is also a key instrument of influence. Irritate an audience with an abrasive delivery and they stop listening to the message. Wrap an average idea in a resonant voice and the idea carries more weight than it should on its own.

Almost all of us have potentially pleasant voices, and can eliminate some features we don't like. We really can't do much about vocal pitch. If we come equipped with long, thick vocal bands, our voices are going to be low. If the vocal folds are relatively small and thin, vocal pitch will be high. In the North American culture, low is considered better. But pitch, which is hard to change, is not as important for persuaders as voice *quality*.

Voice quality is produced by the sound of the vocal bands travelling into the throat, nasal passage and mouth. Sound shooting directly into the nasal passage will have a decidedly nasal twang. Such a twang served Don

Knotts well when he was assistant sheriff on the old Andy Griffith show, but for most, the twang is a turn-off.

The human voice is extremely versatile. Anyone who wants to polish vocal quality can use a tape recorder to improve resonance. Most speakers don't take advantage of the throat, nasal passage and mouth to produce the pleasant sound so essential to a positive ethos. Listening to your voice played back on a tape recorder will reveal quickly whether the sound is tight and consequently non-resonant. Practice in expanding the throat, mouth and nasal passage should produce a more pleasant voice.

Enthusiasm

Like resonance, vocal projection can also be improved with practice. Most speakers believe they sound enthusiastic, but thirty seconds with a tape recorder tells them otherwise. Persuaders can change dull, uninspired sound by listening to their voice and then making efforts to increase inflection and vocal energy.

There's a double benefit in increasing vocal projection during a public talk. The same projection that makes a speaker sound enthusiastic to an audience also harnesses the stagefright most public speakers dread. One of the best public speaking courses I've ever taken was from a man who originally hated giving talks. His name was Art Quine, and he completed the Dale Carnegie course to get over his fear of the platform. Later, he developed his own class designed on the principle that strong voice projection is one of the best ways to keep an audience's attention and also channel nervousness.

Art's classes were fun as well as educational. He had each student give a "fanatic speaker" talk. He told us to prepare a speech on a controversial topic—*e.g.*, ban Walt Disney movies, abolish bow ties, nominate Ferdinand Marcos for the U.S. Senate, *etc.* Each "fanatic" brought a rolled-up newspaper which he was told to smash against the podium at key points in the address. Above all, the instructor insisted that each orator *project* his voice because the audience was instructed to boo and hiss when Art gave the signal. Four students were given the honor of shouting derogatory comments at the speaker. Despite some initial reluctance, most students really plunged into the exercise and learned two valuable lessons: a dynamic delivery is persuasive and vocal energy helps overcome nervousness.

While some speakers project too much and make listeners wince, most aren't energetic enough either during a public talk or private conversation. Listen carefully to Jane Pauley or Mike Wallace as they steer their way through an interview. Their rate is slower than average, and their voices brim with controlled enthusiasm.

Audience Identification

Harry Truman was a master at beginning his talks by referring to events important to the citizens he addressed. Truman would have his advance men go into a 1948 town or city, and find out what was important to the folks who lived there. If Bridgeport, Connecticut, prided itself on a softball team and fine schools, Truman would begin by making references to such sources of civic pride. Like many skilled persuaders, he would tell the audience how pleased he was to be with them and how much he admired their city.

Either by instinct or careful study, successful motivators mirror the voice cadence and body rhythm of the people they encounter. If their conversation partner speaks rapidly, so do they. If the other person has an animated delivery, they do too. If the client crosses his legs, so does the persuader. Neuro-linguistic advocates suggest this method of mirroring as an effective sales tool. In addition to matching emotional moods, the adept motivator will literally imitate mannerisms and bodily motions of the client. While this may seem extremely obvious, it's usually not to the person being imitated.

Rapport

Why do we like some people instantly and have to put on our best acting job with others in order to appear civil? Not everyone clicks with everybody else. But some are adept at establishing and maintaining an easy rapport which makes them highly effective as motivators. They establish an interpersonal synchrony with most people they meet. How do they do it?

Rapport with people is most often related to how others treat us. Put simply, we generally like people who like us, think the way we do and have similar interests. Salespeople capitalize on these factors as they try to establish and maintain rapport with customers. If we've been to Yellowstone Park, so have they. If we hate dishwashers that break down, so do they. If we confide that the Denver Broncos are the greatest team in America, we hear "Hey, they're my team too! Go Broncos!" The adept seller immediately gets on our wavelength and rides it for the duration of the pitch.

Politicians kiss babies, beam their smile around the room, and tell us they're really glad to meet us because they know that the simple act of liking someone is enough to gain a vote. Millions know little about political issues but know who they like and dislike. The knee-jerk reaction of liking often pulls in more votes than a candidate's ideas and political stance.

Successful motivators get us to like them by liking us first. Dale Carnegie was one of the first to suggest the compliment as a tool of persuasion. Few can resist the seduction of praise. Sure, sometimes the shrewd observer can tell the difference between flattery and praise, but most find the deftly expressed positive remark disarming. The persuader weaves her way into our heart and mind by praising a deed we've done or an outfit we're wearing. We glow for a moment and the stage is set for influence. This is not to suggest that everyone who hands out a compliment is also trying to get something in return. Undisguised flattery can have a boomerang effect if the recipient believes he's being conned. But sincere praise creates a liking bond between giver and receiver and establishes an important predisposition for persuasion.

Humor and Rapport

One proven device for establishing rapport is humor. When a reporter challenged John Kennedy at a press conference about his decision to appoint his brother attorney general, the President responded, "I see nothing wrong with giving Robert some legal experience before he goes out and practices law."

On another occasion, a reporter stated: "The Republican National Committee passed a resolution stating that you were pretty much a failure, how do you feel about that?" Kennedy replied, "I assume it passed unanimously."[10]

Like other successful persuaders, Kennedy used a quick wit and well-timed sense of humor to maintain a bond with his listeners. As a result, his attractiveness soared as did his ability to persuade. Ronald Reagan has been able to deflect criticism with the quick quip and the Irish twinkle in his eye. We like leaders who don't take themselves too seriously and are willing to poke fun at themselves. We dislike the pompous and overly serious. Someone once said that the higher the leader goes on the flagpole of leadership, the more he leaves exposed. If humor is the shortest distance between two people, it's one of the most effective means of persuading others. Humorous people exude warmth and are fun to be around.

Skilled motivators use humor as a tool for diffusing volatile situations. In trying to tone down a tense situation, one college president told the story of the man who had challenged the quality of college education today. He said the person asked the question, "Why is it that 80 percent of our college students today can't write, and the other 35 percent can't do simple math?"

Notre Dame coach Louis Holtz is known as "The Quipper." He's a hard-driving perfectionist who knows how to balance discipline with humor. Football players and almost anyone else will put up with a strong leader who can make them laugh.

Charisma: A Special Category

He was the kind of speaker who could talk about water drainage and make it fascinating. Without trying, Dominic LaRusso electrified a room the instant he walked in. When I first met him, he was a professor at the University of Washington and had just returned from a sabbatical leave. Graduate students gathered to hear him talk about his year of research in Europe. As he spoke, it was clear that he was eloquent and well organized. But Dominic LaRusso had something extra—he exuded charisma.

Some have it but most don't. Try to define charisma and the words slip away like quicksilver. But certain qualities stand out. Charismatic figures project energy. Most are excellent actors who can glide from anger to sorrow to laughter within a span of four minutes and take their listeners with them on the ride. Charismatic speakers have a well cultivated flair for the dramatic which rivets the attention of listeners and sweeps them along toward acceptance of whatever ideas are presented.

Charisma is to ethos what Placido Domingo is to John Denver. They're both great entertainers but one has a vocal gift the other doesn't. The *American College Dictionary* defines charisma as "a divinely conferred gift or power" and "those special spiritual powers of personal qualities that give an individual authority over large numbers of people."[11] Jay Conger wrote his doctoral dissertation on the subject and concluded that charisma can be taught to a certain degree.[12] He maintains that charismatic motivators are unconventional and are willing to take more risks than others: "They have a rather profound sense of strategic vision, and they are very good at articulating that vision." Charismatic motivators are more emotional than most people and paint vivid, emotion-laden images for their audience. Their delivery is more dramatic than most orators. While not everyone can go from a bland, unexciting plodder to an electrifying spell-binder, most leaders can turn on more emotion in situations which call for it.

Urban II and Martin Luther King had charisma. So did Adolf Hitler and Jim Jones. Mary Kay of cosmetic fame has charisma and wields it not only to sell her products, but also to give her sales representatives a stronger self-image and greater enthusiasm in their lives. Charisma is a cut above ethos and is one of the key factors in explaining why persuasion works so well with some audiences. Charismatic speakers captivate, compel and excite crowds with their vision and talent for transmitting that vision. Their energy and intense personal appeal is often the main reason for their astounding success.

Summary of Key Points

1. Personal appeal is crucial to persuasion. Most people can sharpen their ethos by careful cultivation of the image they project. Such an image should telegraph competence, integrity and rapport.

2. Personal appeal is more a product of how motivators relate to their audience rather than physical attractiveness. Successful motivators exude warmth to their listeners and most listeners respond in kind.

3. Perceived integrity is the most important facet of persuasion. If an audience doesn't believe or trust a motivator, very little else a speaker does will work.

4. *Who* persuades is often as crucial as the message. Listeners will respond positively to speakers they consider experts on the subject.

5. Most effective persuaders have worked hard to gain a thorough knowledge of their subject and are able to project such an impression to their listeners.

6. The right clothes enhance a speaker's credibility and personal appeal. Audiences often make judgements about speakers on looks alone. Knowing this, adept motivators dress carefully for the occasion and audience.

7. The human voice is a key instrument in persuading. But most people don't know how they sound. Therefore they would benefit from a systematic program which lets them hear their voice the way others hear it. The program should also include regular practice with a tape recorder to make best use of vocal energy and quality.

8. Successful persuaders get on the emotional and rational wavelength of an audience. They often mirror the physical gestures of their listeners because people tend to be more influenced by those who are like them and hold the same ideas.

9. Charisma is a special category. Few persuaders can mesmorize an audience, but most can sharpen their personal appeal by projecting enthusiasm and warmth.

3

The Emotional Hook

I've come to call it the "sock talk" and remember it as one of the most powerful speeches I've ever heard. The speaker was a football coach trying to convince his high school charges to go out and win the big game. "Marv" was a motivator who knew how to push the right buttons. As a new teacher at an all-boys Catholic school, I had the job of helping with the football equipment—an assignment that provided the chance to see one of the region's great persuaders in action.

The "sock talk" turned out to be Marv's finest effort and he wisely chose to save his pyrotechnics for the biggest game of the season. The year before, his squad had lost a very close championship game because a speedy half-back on the other team had scored the winning TD just before the final gun. The young man had forgotten one of his stockings in the jubilant celebration that followed victory. Marv's smallish sophomore manager approached him and showed him the sock. He told the coach he would wash it and then return it to the other team. Marv saw a golden opportunity and the perfect symbol for next year's game. "No," he said, "we'll keep it and I'll use it later." The sock remained unwashed and it started taking on a life of its own over the next 12 months.

Finally, the day of the crucial game dawned—crisp, cold and clear. After a stirring pep rally, Marv gathered his team together to work his motivational magic. All the games produced unforgettable rhetorical gems, but Marv outdid himself this time. He began by holding the sock for all to see. Starting softly but gathering momentum as he spoke, he snarled, "Here is the sock that beat you guys last year. It was worn by the same halfback who scored the winning touchdown—the same guy who'll be out there tonight ready to do it again. Do you know what he did last year? After the game, he came into the locker room and threw this sock in the face of our five-foot manager and shouted, 'Here's the sock that ran all over you guys.' " The fact that no such conversation took place didn't stop Marv as he used poetic license to hammer home his points.

The coach then threw the sock at his biggest tackle. The lineman couldn't bear holding the symbol of defeat, so he tossed it to a half-back—who threw it to someone else. As the sock traveled around the room, the players became more enraged. After the item of ignominy had made its rounds, the team rose in mass indignation and ran out the door on their way to victory.

Most of us have been mesmerized at one time or another by an emotional speaker. As we sat listening to the message, we got angry, fearful, jubilant or depressed. And often, the feeling was not rational. It wasn't reasonable for the young football players to get mad over a sock. It may not be logical for a well practiced worrier to hear a talk about the dangers of UFOs and then to fret himself into a state of near collapse. It may be irrational to spin into a state of blue funk because our favorite NFL team lost the game that kept them out of the playoffs. But that's the problem with emotions—they often don't make sense because they're feelings.

For centuries, philosophers have tried to explain the difference between reason and emotion and have found it a difficult task. Some have separated reason from feelings by fitting them into compartments of the mind: one part of the brain is the cradle of thought and another houses human emotional responses. Even though today's neuroscientists have isolated emotions to a place on the right side of the brain in the limbic section, they still admit to knowing little about human emotional responses.[1] The study of the human mind is still in its infancy, but we know that emotions are often the catalysts for behavior. For this reason, they're powerful sources of motivation.

We all come equipped with the same basic set of human needs, but emotions vary from person to person. I may melt when I hear a recording of Bing Crosby singing "White Christmas" on December 24 while you may think the song is corny and are left unmoved. Rock music by Van Halen creates disgust in one person and elation in another. One penitent can listen to a sermon on sin and be consumed by guilt while another yawns as he thinks about breakfast. The successful persuader tries to discover the exact emotions of her audience so she can address them. Tapping into those emotions can mean the difference between failure or success because emotional appeal is often more effective than the rational. As much as people claim they make decisions based on reason, frequently they respond to satisfy an emotional need.

Abraham Maslow provides the best known explanation of human needs. Maslow divides needs into a five-layered triangle. (See model below)

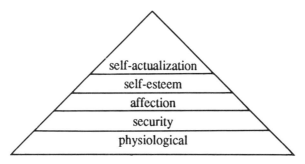

There are two reasons Maslow uses the triangle. First, the lower needs have to be satisfied before the higher ones can be met. Second, the lower ones are satisfied more often. Someone can never miss a meal, but feels a lack of love in his life. Or someone else may get plenty of praise and affection, but deep down is frustrated in her pursuit to actualize herself as an artist.

The best persuaders are those who take the time to discover which specific needs are most dominant in their listeners. Successful motivators also probe to find out the intensity of emotions in their audience. If the promoter of the Health Spa knows that a potential customer feels deeply depressed about his body shape, his job of getting new members is made easier. If the basketball coach knows that her starting players have a deep sense of pride and self-esteem, she can do a better job of motivating them to win.

Why an Emotional Appeal Is Often More Powerful Than a Logical One

In *Mein Kampf,* Adolf Hitler underscored the advantage of the spoken word over the written. He also emphasized that emotional appeal has greater impact than logical, especially on the masses.[2] Hitler followed his own advice as he convinced thousands of Germans to follow him on one of the most tragic journeys in world history. Much of Hitler's power, especially in the early years of the Third Reich, was created through a series of public speeches aimed at the emotions of the masses. The emotional appeal shrouded some of the most illogical and heinous ideas of this or any other century, but such an appeal struck a chord in many a listener.

Hitler knew that a number of Germans felt humiliated by their loss of the First World War and were depressed about their sagging economy. Therefore, he played on those themes in a series of highly-charged speeches. Hitler and his propaganda minister Joseph Goebbels spent the equivalent of a million dollars a day to motivate Nazi soldiers during the war.[3]

For many, an emotional appeal works better than one loaded with logic and supporting evidence. Why? By their very nature, emotions evoke feelings. And the stronger the feeling, the more likely an immediate response. Most people don't get excited by logic. They nod and agree that mathematical principles or logical syllogisms make sense and let it go at that. Not so with emotions. Emotions make listeners want to shout, stand, take over and *do something.* Notice the emotional impact of Mark Antony's speech to the Roman mob after the death of Julius Caesar.

Even though the speeches by Brutus and Mark Antony never occurred exactly the way Shakespeare crafted them in *Julius Caesar*, the two orations stand in sharp contrast as models of the logical and emotional approach. Mark Antony's tribute to Caesar serves as a cogent example of how a speaker who laces his talk with emotion will win out over someone who appeals mainly to reason.

Brutus, who spoke first, was steady and rational as he tried to convince his hearers that the assassination was justified. His arguments roll out like a parade of syllogisms:

Not that I loved Caesar less, but that I loved Rome more. Had you rather Caesar were living and die all slaves, than that Caesar were dead, to live all free men? As Caesar loved me, I weep for him; as he was fortunate, I rejoice at it; as he was valiant, I honor him; but as he was ambitious, I slew him.[4]

After a few more words, Brutus pauses and then asks if he has offended anyone. No one responds to his methodical explanation for the killing. Who could argue with such logic?

The conspirators then allow Mark Antony to speak because they believe he'll support their reasons for eliminating Caesar. Little did they know that Caesar's friend was setting a rhetorical trap. His opening famous lines lull them into a false sense of complacency: "I come to bury Caesar, not to praise him. The evil that men do lives after them. The good is oft interred with their bones. So let it be with Caesar." Mark Antony sounds sincere as he points out that "Brutus is an honorable man. So are they all, all honorable men." But this phrase will soon twist and turn Antony's message from one of apparent support to bitter irony.

Mark Antony knew how to work a crowd. With a skillful blend of irony, sarcasm and pity, he started slowly and then built his speech to a fever pitch. He asks the crowd if Caesar was ambitious when he filled the public coffers, wept with the poor and three times turned down the crown. Antony then tells the citizens about Caesar's will but asks them not to force him to read it because it will turn them against these "honorable men." The crowd screams to hear the will and Antony responds by telling them that it will only make them mad to hear how much Caesar loved them.

But before disclosing the contents of Caesar's will, the speaker asks the Roman audience to look closely at the bloody body of their leader and to ponder the brutality of the wounds. And then he underscores the "unkindest cut of all": Brutus was Caesar's friend who betrayed him. The betrayal by these honorable men "quite vanquished him: then burst his mighty heart." Antony then tells the citizens that Caesar has left 75 drachmas to each of them. He has also bequeathed his walks, private gardens and newly-planted orchards.

Antony's speech so incensed the crowd that they chased Brutus and the other conspirators into the streets and torched their houses. As often happens in real life, emotion wins out over reason because it gets the adrenalin flowing. Bored listeners sit and nod in agreement at the logical speech. Emotion-charged oratory impels action.

The Appeal to Fear: High and Low

Rage is only one of an array of emotions a speaker can use to work a crowd. Fear is another. Students who attended a Jesuit high school in the 1950s and 60s almost certainly participated in a two-day retreat conducted by a motivational Jesuit. As part of that experience, the preacher gave a talk on hell that had all of us vowing to change our lives. One sermon in particular stands out in my mind as the all-time fear provoker. After describing in graphic detail the horrible burning sensation of fire and brimstone, the speaker pulled out one of his most dramatic analogies to give us adolescents some notion of eternity. He asked us to picture in our mind the sun as a huge lead ball. He then invited us to imagine a little bird flying to the sun every 100 years and brushing its wings against the big lead ball. With his voice rising to a dramatic plateau, he asked us, "How many years would it take the bird to completely brush away the entire sun if the bird made his trip every century?" Pausing for proper emphasis, the speaker then proclaimed, "Even after the bird had completely rubbed away the lead sun after millions of years, eternity *would have just begun!*"

Most of us got the message and trembled as we pondered eternity. But there was a problem—the fear didn't last. When people listen to a message loaded with strong fear appeals, they're motivated at the moment because the speaker has stimulated such intense feelings. Precisely because the message is so horrible, most listeners banish it from their minds as soon as they can.

Years later, I heard another explanation of hell which was far more effective in changing my attitude even though the fear appeal was moderate. During an eight-day retreat, Fr. Frank Marion, another Jesuit, gave a different version of eternal punishment. Instead of focusing on fire and brimstone, he had the retreatants consider the nature of God as a loving Supreme being who has given human beings free will. From a Christian perspective, happiness depends on a loving relationship with someone besides ourselves. To be fulfilled, we need to reach out to others.

With free will, we can get in the habit of choosing ourselves if we want—much like the depressing hero of Albert Camus' short novel *The Fall*. In the book, a successful Parisian lawyer admits that he lives for himself. He has chosen to stay unmarried because he doesn't want to be restricted in his pursuit of pleasure. He helps the blind cross the street, not because he wants to serve them, but because the charitable act makes him feel good.

One night, after leaving the apartment of his mistress, he starts home and crosses one of the many bridges that span the Seine river. Halfway across, he notices a young woman gazing despondently into the dark, churning waters below. He walks on until the quiet night is broken by the sound of a splash. Within seconds, he hears cries of help and starts to move back to save the young woman. But he stops. The thought of the cold water and the trouble involved makes him turn and walk away. This is the denouement of the story. Camus' character has become so ingrained in the habit of choosing himself, that he can't reach out to someone else.

Camus' story reinforced an image of hell not as a place of intense pain inflicted by God, but one of utter loneliness endured by someone who has sought only self. Self-centeredness is a habit and like any other deeply reinforced habit, it is hard to break. The person who constantly seeks himself comes to the point of facing God and God says, "Here I am." The self-centered individual says, in effect, "No, I would rather have myself." God honors this decision and thus hell becomes eternal loneliness, utter isolation. On the other hand, someone who chooses others over self finds it much easier to establish union with God both in this life and the next. Such a person is "other-oriented" and is in the habit of reaching outward instead of turning constantly to self.

While not everyone would be affected as I was by this explanation, the two versions of hell confirmed for me the impact of the low fear appeal. The fire and brimstone, small bird versus lead ball analogy had us trembling for a time, but its effect was short-lived. The explanation of hell as total loneliness made more sense. The fear of utter aloneness didn't create the same sense of terror as the traditional "give 'em what hell's like and make 'em shiver" sermon, but in the long run, it had more staying power.

The enduring quality of the low fear appeal was demonstrated in an experiment conducted a few years ago. A state highway patrol wanted to influence teen-agers not to mix drinking and driving. To accomplish this, the patrol produced a film which depicted horrible car crashes complete with twisted metal on a blood-drenched highway. The visual impact was reinforced by dramatic music.

The producers of the film were pleased with audience reactions as high school students squirmed and gasped during the showing. If the movie was shown just before lunch, many of the students couldn't eat, especially if the cafeteria was serving tomato soup that day. But did the film work in convincing its targets to avoid drinking and driving? No. Although the movie created a strong and immediate emotional reaction, most of the viewers tried to banish the images as quickly as they could because they were so repulsive.

A less dramatic but more effective film featured a highway patrolman stopping a teenager and handing out a ticket for $95. For a repeat offense, the culprit's driver's license was revoked for a year. The lower fear appeal worked better than the high-intensity, blood and gore approach.

Guilt

Erma Bombeck has noted that "guilt is the gift that keeps on giving." Guilt can also be a potent emotional tool for the persuader. Some humans may have escaped the feeling of guilt, but most have experienced it often. Like other emotions, guilt can be rational or irrational. Anyone with a normal conscience who steals from his neighbor or cheats on his income tax will feel guilty. But often, people endure guilt for no good reason. A 33-year old woman may be plagued by remorse because her mother waits up for her until 2 a.m. rather than going to bed. And even though the young woman can tell herself that her mother *chooses* to keep her sacrificial vigil, the feeling remains. Despite the daughter's insistence that her mother go to bed, mother replies, "That's all right. I'll just wait up for you until you come in—no matter what that hour might be." The daughter should logically conclude, "That's your choice, Mom. Go ahead and wait up." But logic doesn't count here. The daughter feels a force all evening that pushes her to get home at 1 a.m. rather than 2:30 because she can't stand the guilt.

Carried to an extreme, guilt can produce one of the most painful human experiences—scruples. Some people are plagued with the conviction that no matter what they do, they're incurring God's wrath. They accidently step on a rosary or look at what they consider a lewd picture, and they're consumed with intense guilt. They can't sleep or find a moment's relief. The pressure to find peace is so great that they'll do almost anything to remove the burden. This also makes them highly susceptible to a persuader who can offer release from the scruples.

Relieving Dissonance

Psychologists have come to refer to guilt and other forms of mental uneasiness as "cognitive dissonance"—a term coined by Leon Festinger. Few people can stay in turmoil for very long; most will do almost anything to regain peace of mind. Scruples and worry are two examples of cognitive dissonance. The concept is important in persuasion because successful motivators play on dissonance to achieve their purpose. Dissonance is the troubled conviction that we've said something that hurt the feelings of a good friend. Dissonance is also "buyer's remorse"—the realization that we've spent way more money than we should on a stereo system or a vacation. Dissonance is the gnawing guilt that we haven't spent enough time with our children.

Like other emotions, dissonance can be reasonable or unreasonable. But reasonable or not, the *feelings* can be strong and need release. Knowing this, the persuader can either try to increase or reduce an audience's dissonance depending on the situation. If the home buyers have shown strong interest in a house and like everything about the deal except the mortgage payment of $650 per month, the adept salesperson doesn't try to argue the point. Instead, she looks for ways to reduce their sense of uneasiness. After agreeing that $650 is $150 over what they wanted to pay per month, she might ask them, "Do you have a savings account?" She hears that they do and that they put around $200 per month into the account. She then suggests that they put $150 into their house instead of the bank and look upon the transaction as a wise investment and a better way of saving. She points out that real estate is one of the most stable investments and, even despite slips, the home buyer usually comes out ahead. Why let the $200 per month sit in the bank and draw a low-yield 8 percent, when they can apply $150 to the mortgage and realize a profit when they want to sell the house? Without skipping a beat or losing her smile, she tells them they'll not only *make money* but also have the home they *really* want.

On the other hand, a persuader may want to *increase* uneasiness for an audience. In the delightful Meredith Wilson production *The Music Man*, Harold Hill stirs up strong concern over the presence of a pool table in

River City. Few parents had worried that such a device was leading their children down the path of corruption, but Professor Hill was able to create just such a feeling of uneasiness. With flair and flourish, the persuader took an item that caused no concern before and made it a source of anxiety. The negative pitch on the pool hall was a prelude to his main purpose of selling the town on the band he would lead.

The Language of Emotion

The young politician was in trouble. Even though he was the vice-presidential candidate on one of the strongest tickets in American history, Richard Nixon had to explain himself in September of 1952. Nixon had been the point-man for the Republican ticket and had skewered his Democratic rivals. Partly in retaliation, opponents accused him of having a secret campaign fund of $18,000 which he allegedly was using for his personal needs. After meticulous preparation and some shrewd audience analysis, Nixon answered his critics in a speech on September 23, 1952. The nationally televised talk has come to be called the "Checkers" speech. What the oration lacked in logic, it made up for in its successful impact through emotional appeal. Nixon didn't focus on the use of the campaign fund as much as he zeroed in on the hearts of his massive audience.

The unabashed emotional appeal worked far better than a detailed explanation of what happened to the $18,000. Nixon used specific, graphic and heart-tugging language. Instead of talking in abstractions, he explained how he and Pat had scrimped and saved to live like most young, American families. They had their debts but through hard work, had managed to save a little money. Near the end, he looked directly at the viewers and used the tactic that gave the speech its name. After listing his financial assets and liabilities, he said:

> Well, that's about it. That's what we have. That's what we owe. It isn't very much, but Pat and I have the satisfaction that every dime that we've got is honestly ours. I should say this—that Pat doesn't have a mink coat. But she does have a respectable

Republican cloth coat. And I always tell her that she'd look good in anything.

One other thing I probably should tell you because if I don't, they'll probably be saying this about me, too. We did get something—a gift—after the election (nomination). A man down in Texas heard Pat on the radio mention the fact that our two youngsters would like to have a dog. And, believe it or not, the day before we left on this campaign trip, we got a message from Union Station in Baltimore saying they had a package for us. We went down to get it. You know what it was.

It was a little cocker spaniel dog in a crate that he had sent all the way from Texas. Black and white spotted. And our little girl—Tricia, the six-year-old—named it Checkers. And you know, the kids love the dog and I just want to say this right now, that regardless of what they say about it, we're going to keep it.[5]

What granite-souled viewer could dare suggest that Tricia couldn't keep the dog? Who could resist the picture of a young breadwinner who loved his wife and kids? Many a tear was wiped away that evening as Nixon closed his talk. The speech brought in two million positive telegrams, phone calls and letters. It saved Nixon's career at a pivotal time and kept him on the ticket.

Feeling Obligated

I want to confess a peculiar quirk. If someone sends me a thank-you note, I feel obligated to thank that person for the thank-you. A few seconds' reflection tells me that I really don't have to do this, but the compulsion to respond is there. And if someone gives me anything—a free sample of toothpaste, three days' worth of mouthwash, a brochure, or their time—I have an urge to give something back. Cialdini refers to this universal feeling as the "rule of reciprocation" and identifies it as a key factor in influencing others. To make the point, he cites the example of a university professor who sent out a number of Christmas cards to total strangers. What happened? Almost all who received a card sent one back, even though they had no idea of who the benevolent stranger was.[6]

The adage "Tis better to give than receive" applies in persuasion. Most people feel better about themselves when they're giving rather than receiving. Giving usually brings a "no-strings attached" kind of joy. But to *receive* generates an "I've got to give something back" feeling. Knowing this, a business gives away anything from a free sample of food at the supermarket to a year's car rental. Motivators who cast their bread on the waters of human feeling almost always get back more than they give.

How Not to Persuade

The tactic of the insult might work for Don Rickles in getting laughs, but backfires in persuasion because it goes against one of the deepest human emotions—the need to preserve self-esteem. Put someone down and he immediately feels compelled to muster all of his psychic forces to protect himself. The scathing rebuke may be a therapeutic release for the one who delivers it but almost always fails in changing attitudes. In fact, the caustic comment creates a boomerang effect in the receiver.

A nation or an individual with absolute power can use force to get results. But if we want to motivate someone, we try to avoid the self-righteous, negative frontal attack. Let's say we're driving through the middle of town when two teen-age males walk directly in front of our car. Consumed with righteous indignation that they're violating the law, we lay on the horn for a good five seconds. What is their reaction? Do they stop and bow in profound apology? Do they come up to the window of the car and say "Hey, look, we forgot we're not supposed to jaywalk. Please excuse us. We won't let it happen again." No, their response is to emphatically raise their right hands with half of the victory sign and shout a string of obscenities. Instead of walking faster to get out of the way, they slow to a saunter.

Attack someone's self-esteem and he does the opposite of what we want. That approach sometimes works with small children and dogs but not with most humans. Walk up to a smoker who is clearly breaking the law by lighting up in a supermarket or restaurant. Point out to him the error of his ways and we usually get a variety of responses—all negative. Sometimes the smoker glares. At other times, he blows smoke in the chider's face. There are cases where non-smoking and smoking passengers flying together get into a physical fight. Self-esteem is a strong emotion and most people will do almost anything to protect it.

At first glance, Christ's directive of not resisting violence and turning the other cheek seems hard. If we're pushed, we want to push back. But the non-violent response has a far better chance of working with most people than the counterattack. If we smile and wave at the teenagers crossing in front of the car, their response is usually positive. The gentle, loving comeback is not only a surprise to the offender—it often turns his wrath to receptivity. And such receptivity opens the door to persuasion.

Summary of Key Points

1. Appeals to emotion are often more effective than ones to reason because emotions are feelings. Feelings, in turn, make people want to act.

2. Emotional responses vary from person to person. Successful motivators identify the specific emotions of their audience and adapt their persuasive appeal to those emotions.

3. High fear appeals produce immediate strong reactions, but precisely because the feeling is so unpleasant, people tend to get rid of them as soon as they can. Therefore, low-fear appeals often have more staying power.

4. Adept persuaders capitalize on cognitive dissonance to meet their goal. Depending on the circumstance, they either try to increase or decrease it in their listeners.

5. Specific language which depicts strong emotional images has more impact than abstract words which are hard to picture.

6. People who feel obligated through some gift or favor are compelled to give something back. Hence, persuaders give with the sure knowledge that they'll get something in return.

7. Unless an individual holds great power over someone else, insults and criticism don't work but often make the recipient want to do the opposite of what the persuader wants.

4

Appeal to Reason

For two years, an unknown rapist roamed the parks and jogging trails of Spokane, Washington. Over 30 women were attacked, as citizens and police alike were stymied in their efforts to stop the assaults. The *Spokesman Review* and *Chronicle* newspapers combined forces to encourage people to report any information that might lead to an arrest. Finally, on March 10, 1981, detectives arrested a 34-year-old real estate agent by the name of Fred Coe. The city was stunned because the accused was the son of the *Chronicle's* editor, Gordon Coe.

The Coe trials are presented here not to dredge up a case that most people would like to forget, but to illustrate how logical argument is used as a persuasive tool. The American court system is one of the last bastions where the participants must adhere to rules of reason. If they don't, they stand little chance of winning since judges apply rules of logic and evidence as their criteria in making decisions.

The court insists on reason over emotion for at least two reasons: (1) adhering to rules of logical argument and evidence provides the best chance of achieving justice and (2) while each person's idea of what is logical is somewhat different, emotion is much more subjective. What moves me to tears may bore you. But, most of the time, we can come close on agreeing that someone indicted for a crime is either guilty or innocent based on the amount of evidence. If the evidence shows, beyond a reasonable doubt, that the accused is guilty, then we as jurors will probably agree to convict. If a case has insufficient evidence, we'll most likely acquit. The closer we can come to the ideal of mathematical or logical certainty, the better the chance that justice will be done.

Patricia Thompson, the Deputy Prosecutor in the Coe trials,[1] has spoken three times to my persuasion classes about the place of logical argument in a court case. Pat Thompson stands five foot three and at first glance looks like she's 23 years old. But when she talks in her animated and articulate style, no one doubts her skills as a motivator. In her presentation to the class, she explains the persuasive strategy she used in getting convictions against a man who looks more like the recipient of the "Young Executive of the Year" award than a rapist.

Coe's Background

Coe grew up in Spokane on the city's southside where he graduated from Lewis and Clark High School. He later dropped out of college and made his way to Las Vegas where he worked as a disco deejay. After a failed marriage and some time in California, Coe returned to Spokane and got his license as a real estate agent. But instead of selling houses, he spent most of his time on a one-man public relations project he called Spokane Metro Growth. He also sat at his typewriter for hours grinding out material he hoped to publish. But, according to the case brought against him by the Spokane County Prosecutor's Office, Coe was also attacking women on the city's southside. From 1978 to 1981, Spokane women lived in fear of a six-foot jogger who casually ran toward his prey, passed her and then turned around to strike. Victims ranged in age from 15 to 51 and all of them described a man with a mellow voice who peppered his gruesome conversation with explicit sexual language.

After a woman was raped near a Spokane junior high school in February of 1980, a janitor at the school noticed a late model silver Chevrolet Citation and called the Spokane Police. An officer traced the car to Gordon Coe, the managing editor of the *Chronicle*. The senior Coe had loaned his son the Citation. Rather than making an arrest immediately, police attached a small homing device to the fender of the car and followed

Coe for three weeks. They watched him leave early in the morning and drive along the same route on South Hill. He occasionally stopped and stared at women joggers. One detective said, "It looked like he was trolling for victims."

On a bright Sunday morning in early March, a man in a jogging suit approached a woman runner near Washington Water Power, Spokane's main utility company. As he passed, the man spouted obscene comments and brandished a plastic dildo. The day before, someone had stolen the young woman's bicycle and she was so infuriated by this second affront in two days that she started chasing the man. He jumped into a silver Citation and roared into the Sunday sunlight. She quickly flagged a passing motorist who pursued the Citation until the car swerved into a Washington Water Power parking lot. The driver then slipped out and hid in some bushes until a security guard came toward him. Acting as if this were normal procedure for a Sunday morning, the man in the bushes got up, brushed off his sweatsuit, murmured "good morning" to the guard, slid into his car, and drove away. Police made the connection between the silver Citation at the junior high school and the one at the utility company. The next day, they arrested Coe at his real estate office.

After the arrest, Coe's parents began a long, impassioned and unwavering defense of their son. Both claimed that the Spokane Police were under so much pressure to find a suspect that they had picked on an innocent and upright citizen. Members of Coe's family were the only ones to stand behind him through both trials. The first trial began in July of 1981 with a jury transported from the Seattle area. The case had produced such a strong community response and had been so widely publicized, that it became impossible to find twelve people in Spokane who had not heard about the crimes.

The case for the prosecution was not easy. Despite using female officers as decoys, Spokane police couldn't catch the assailant in the act. Also, the rapist struck in the dark and was careful to hide his face from his victims. The accused didn't look anything like the stereotypical rapist as he sat in court and faced the jury. His three-piece suits, well-trimmed hair and boyish sincerity made it difficult to believe that Coe was guilty of anything as heinous as rape. The foreman of the jury in the first trial, David Barkman, described his initial reaction to Coe: "On first impression, I perceived Mr. Coe as a very well-educated, super-fantastic . . . guy. As far as I was concerned, the gentleman was innocent. I couldn't believe a fellow who looked like he did, talked like he did and came from the background he had, could be guilty."[2]

Inductive Logic and Evidence

The prosecutors' major challenge was to convince the jury that someone who looked like Coe could be guilty of rape. Pat Thompson and her fellow prosecutors had to prove their case through inductive arguments supported by evidence. Inductive arguments are based on a series of specific incidents which lead to a general conclusion. Unlike deduction, which begins with an obvious generalization and then moves to a particular conclusion, the inductive approach is the format for most cases in court. To merely claim that Kevin Coe[3] was guilty as charged would be an assertion. And while attorneys can use emotional appeal, they must build their case on the bedrock of reason. Given enough time, most jurors will see how either the evidence leads to a conviction or is so weak that the accused should be set free. In some cases, the jurors can't reach a decision but in most, the system works well and a judgement is made about innocence or guilt.

Even though logical arguments provide the best chance of getting at the truth and insuring justice, jurors see evidence from the perspective of their own attitudes. In a rape trial, one juror might believe that a woman who gets attacked had to be asking for it. Another may be convinced that the victims are completely innocent and did nothing to provoke the attack. Attorneys know that people perceive arguments in different ways. Therefore, during the "voir dire . . ." stage of jury selection, lawyers on both sides try to determine how each prospective juror might see the case.

The prosecution had to make sure that any statements presented during the trial were true, supported by evidence and logically consistent.

Evidence means the difference between an unsubstantiated assertion and a well-supported argument. In the Coe case, the burden of proof was on the prosecution to prove beyond a reasonable doubt that Coe was guilty as charged. The state had to show that the evidence was so conclusive that jurors have little doubt about the guilt of the accused. If, at the end of the trial, jurors have serious doubts about the defendant's guilt, he should be acquitted. If, however, after listening to the arguments, they believe, with a high degree of probability, that the accused is guilty as charged, they should convict. As in other forms of logical persuasion, a jury can't have mathematical certainty, but they can come as close as humanly possible.[4]

Persuaders applying logical argument can draw on at least three kinds of evidence—facts, statistics and testimony. The prosecution sifted through voluminous pieces of evidence to find the ones which would be most persuasive with the jurors. In both trials, testimonial evidence became the cornerstone of the case. The victims and Coe's live-in girl friend turned out to be the most damaging to Coe and ultimately the most persuasive, even though the County relied on factual evidence for back-up support. The assailant had attacked numerous other women, but only six could give the police a line-up identification that would stand up in court. All of the victims told the same story: a man grabbed them from behind and rammed a gloved hand down their throat as he revealed his twisted intentions in a radio announcer voice. Despite his efforts to conceal his face, two of the witnesses were able to look at the attacker.

The prosecution also put on the stand a woman who had lived with Coe for six months. When police went to the rental house she shared with Coe and told her that her boyfriend had been arrested for the South Hill rapes, she connected the pieces of a puzzle that had bothered her for a long time. She finally concluded that her housemate was the notorious rapist the two of them had discussed and whom Coe had vowed to catch himself. On the witness stand, she verified that Coe was an early morning jogger who was often absent during the time of the attacks. Further, he would sometimes come home with torn sweat gear and a scratched face. But particularly telling were a pair of gloves with fingers that became more frayed as the weeks wore on.

In the *Rhetoric,* Aristotle defines persuasion as "finding in a particular case the available means of persuasion." Unlike his mentor, Plato, Aristotle calls persuasion an art because the speaker takes the raw material of evidence and fashions those arguments which will convince an audience. In both Coe trials, Pat Thompson and her colleagues had plenty of evidence—four victims willing to testify, a lack of alibis for the times the rapes took place, computer analysis clearly showing that the four rapes were committed by the same man, plus testimony from Coe's live-in girlfriend that Coe often went jogging at about the same time the victims were attacked. But the challenge was to find the strongest evidence and to skillfully weave it into arguments that would convince the jury. The prosecutors also had to be careful of introducing evidence that might later be overturned by an appeals court.

In the first trial, the defense argued that Coe was not with his girlfriend in the mornings because he was having breakfast with his parents. The accused also vehemently denied that he owned a pair of gloves. But Coe would not admit he had done *anything* wrong—a fact that jury foreman Barker later said turned him against the defendant: "I was left with an impression after he spoke, that he was trying to tell us he was lily white. But nobody is lily white."[5] The prosecution used the parade of victims, the circumstantial evidence of the frayed gloves, the lack of alibi other than from Coe's parents and the defendant's adamant denials of any wrongdoing as the foundation of their case. All of it led to the probable conclusion that Coe was guilty as charged.

Barker and other jurors found Coe guilty and Judge George Shields sentenced him to life plus 75 years in Walla Walla state prison. In 1985, the Washington State Supreme Court overturned the first verdict, primarily on grounds that three of the victims had been hypnotized before they gave testimony in court. The second trial was moved to Seattle in early 1985 and three of the four convictions were upheld and Coe was returned to Walla Walla.[6]

The Difference Between Logic and Human Reason

A court case like Kevin Coe's underscores the value of argumentation in getting at the truth. But using reason in a trial is not the same as applying principles of pure logic or mathematics. Logic and math are certain. Either a syllogism is consistent or it's not. Three plus eight is always eleven and no one is going to argue the point. But in a court case, the issue is not certainty but the *perceptions* of what people believe is reasonable. As Herbert Simons maintains: "One school of philosophers has long maintained that the rules of logic are none other than the laws of human thought; hence to persuade the receiver, one need only present arguments in a logically compelling manner. Unfortunately, this extreme position has found little support from psychological research. At best, the evidence suggests that people seek to . . . obey the rules of their own psycho-logic."[7] Put another way, listeners respond to arguments they *perceive* as rational according to the mind-set they bring to an event involving persuasion. What seems logical to one person may appear outrageous to the next. Knowing this, skillful persuaders probe to discover the attitudes of an audience and then adapt their arguments accordingly. Just as they try to empathize with the feelings of their hearers, they also work to discover what appears rational to the people they're trying to convince.

The highly popular TV and movie series "Star Trek" offered at least one character who made his decisions based on reason alone. Unlike his boss Captain Kirk, Mr. Spock never succumbs to his emotions—except during the Vulcan mating season. At all other times, Spock is open only to reason. While Kirk jeopardizes the Enterprise by falling in love with the Martian princess or reacting to the insulting taunts of Kahn, menacingly played by Ricardo Montalban, Spock keeps his cool. Most people are more like Kirk than Spock. They respond to a combination of emotional and rational appeals. Good persuaders know this and adapt to their audiences. The best attorneys are masters at reading a jury and then lacing their logical arguments with the emotional appeal they believe will touch their listeners. Judges work hard to remind jurors that cases should be decided on evidence and reasoning and not on tugs at the heart.

Using Reason to Persuade

Our court system insists on logic and reason to support claims. So do science and technology. An engineer won't present arguments that a rocket will go into space unless there is rigid proof to insure that it will work. But in many other areas of human experience, persuaders don't have to be logical. Advertisers and salespeople are well aware that consumers often put emotion before reason in buying a product and so they shape their messages accordingly. Ever attuned through motivational research to what customers want, professional persuaders sculpt their messages to fit the buyer. Many consumers buy products to fulfill needs and desires that have little to do with reason.

But there are times when a more logical method works better than an emotional one. In fact, with certain listeners, the strong emotional appeal fizzles and produces the opposite effect the persuader wants. As a group, the hardest to persuade are listeners who have high self-esteem, are well educated and know that complex issues demand complicated solutions. They also view the emotional pitch as highly suspect because they see no evidence to back the claims made by the flamboyant politician, preacher or salesperson. The emotion-drenched talk would boomerang with most attorneys and scientists because they would demand "proof" for any assertions.

Detecting Fallacies

The critical listener looks for fallacies in arguments and won't accept appeals that are not logically sound. An attorney who tries to defend his client with a single isolated piece of evidence, would be committing the fallacy of hasty generalization. So would a researcher who wanted to test how a thousand people felt about a new product and then limited her sample to five. A political candidate who attacks his opponent for a personal trait that has nothing to do with performance in office would be guilty of the *ad hominem* fallacy. The histrionic preacher who appeals only to emotion would be committing the fallacy *ad populum*. Detecting fallacies is a tool the discerning listener applies to insure that arguments have solid evidence and yield logical conclusions.

Besides logical argument in court cases and carefully reasoned strategies for certain audiences, other applications of reason can be applied to persuade. Two of the more practical are the "one-sided, two-sided" approach and "issues over emotion" methods.

The One-sided, Two-sided Approach

I once taught a speech class in Yakima, Washington, during an election. The hottest issue on the ballot was a proposal to add fluoride to the city's water supply to protect children's teeth. One evening, a politically conservative, articulate woman gave an impassioned speech showing how fluoridated water not only turned children's teeth green but would be the first step on the road to socialism. She reasoned that if officials can put fluoride in the water, they can exert other forms of socialistic control. This in turn could lead to communism.

Because she was a very effective speaker, students were persuaded by her arguments. The next week, a nurse who hated giving speeches, utilized an approach called the one-sided versus two-sided method. Her purpose was to counteract the arguments of the anti-fluoridationist. But instead of simply promoting her case, the nurse began by reviewing the points presented by her rhetorical adversary. She said, "Last Tuesday night, you heard our speaker claim that there were two reasons why we should vote against the fluoridation issue. First, you were told that fluoridated water would turn our children's teeth green. Second, you heard that passage of this referendum would mean a step toward socialism. Let me address both arguments."

The speaker went on to say, "It *is* true that children's teeth can turn slightly green if they drink fluoridated water, but they would have to consume 25 bathtubs full of such water in a single sitting. As for the charge that passage of the referendum would mean letting communism creep in, you've probably noticed a small but very vocal group of people who see everything as a communist plot. Marx's grave is a communist plot—excuse the pun—but no one believes it's a threat. The electricity provided for everyone in this area could be construed as a communist plot but no one sees a danger in that." The nurse turned advocate then went on to outline the positive benefits of fluoridated water. These included a guarantee that children would always get their supply of fluoride whether they took pills or not. Furthermore, the low cost of the program would benefit everyone in the area. When she finished, the audience responded with loud applause.

Our reluctant speaker utilized the one-sided, two-sided method of reasoning. Instead of merely stressing her side of the controversial question, she outlined first her opponent's arguments and then dissected them. This approach works better because an audience opposed to a particular position will mentally refute anything the speaker says that goes counter to their stand. But if a speaker begins by reviewing the counter-position, and then refutes it on her own terms, the audience is more open to change. Since the anti-fluoridationist had argued forcefully for her views, class members tended to be against or neutral toward the referendum. The nurse didn't convert her opponent from the week before, but she changed the attitudes of her audience.

Kennedy's Catholicism
and the Two-sided Approach

John Kennedy applied this strategy to convince a group of ministers—and a large number of skeptical voters—that a Catholic president would not owe allegiance to the Pope. As early as the 1960 West Virginia Primary, Kennedy had to deal with his Catholicism in a tough fight with Hubert Humphrey. And while he defeated Humphrey in the primary, this nagging issue wouldn't fade. A group calling itself the National Conference of Citizens for Religious Freedom publicly maintained that Kennedy could not be loyal to his church and his country.[8]

Since most of the opposition came from Southern Protestant ministers, Kennedy addressed the Greater Houston Ministerial Association on September 12. Instead of presenting only his side of the case, Kennedy began the speech by citing the fears he knew were in the minds of the ministers. He was well aware that feelings ran deep about a Catholic in the White House. He also realized that despite his efforts to concentrate on larger issues such as poverty at home and communism abroad, his religion had become a burr in the hide of the campaign. He emphasized that Americans face critical issues such as communism in Cuba, hungry children in West Virginia, old people who can't pay their doctor bills, and families who are forced to give up their farms. Then he went on to say, "But because I am a Catholic, and no Catholic has ever been elected president, the real issues in this campaign have been obscured—perhaps deliberately."[9]

Kennedy then emphatically stated that he believed in absolute separation of church and state. He identified and empathized with the predominantly Protestant audience's views by stating that he too would be appalled by any religious body which would seek to "impose its will directly or indirectly on the general populace."[10] Like them, he would not be in favor of a president who would try to subvert the First Amendment's guarantees of religious liberty. He said, "And I hope that you and I condemn with equal fervor those nations which deny their presidency to Protestants and those which deny it to Catholics."[11] Then in a subtle but important shift of language, Kennedy maintained, "I am not the Catholic candidate for president, I am the Democratic party's candidate for president who happens also to be a Catholic."[12] He then assured audience members that, as president, his criterion for any decision would be the national interest, not outside religious pressure.

By spelling out the fears in the minds of his audience and then directly addressing those fears, Kennedy had a far better chance of winning his hearers than if he had simply stated his own position. If the speaker doesn't bring up an objection, the audience will do it for themselves. Without the one-sided, two-sided approach, listeners mentally refute every point that is not consistent with their own. But when the speaker explains clearly and seems to empathize with their position, a tough issue usually gets diffused.

Issues over Emotions

Because emotions are so strong and often irrational, the successful persuader tries to get a listener to focus on issues rather than feelings. If two sides in a dispute begin by publicly announcing that they will not bend to their opponents, settlement is a long way off because each side is now dealing with a sense of pride in not backing down. Let's say faculty are negotiating with administrators to gain a six percent annual salary increase. If the faculty begins by announcing their six percent stand, they have made a public commitment which will be very difficult to alter in the future. If, at the same time the administration publicly proclaims it will go no higher than four percent, they've also carved their position in granite. Granite can be chiselled and chipped and ultimately changed, but the public commitment makes it difficult because there are now two items involved: the issue of the salary, plus the stand each side takes.

Taking a stand on anything involves ego, self-esteem and pride—all emotional drives. Most negotiations ultimately get worked out, but not before long, tedious hours of wrangling. The key factor that keeps meetings going on far into the night and the next day is the stated commitment by the participants. If a union boss vows to a group of followers that he will never back down and give in to management demands, he'll find it much harder to retreat and admit that he had to compromise to get a fair settlement. When Americans and Soviets publicly proclaim to their citizens that they will stick to a position, negotiations will automatically stretch out because it's hard to back down and save face. The 1987 NFL players strike was almost certainly prolonged because union leaders maintained that they would not give in on the free-agent issue. Owners were just as adamant they would not budge.

In their book *Getting to Yes: Negotiating Agreement Without Giving In,* Roger Fisher and William Ury emphasize the importance of separating issues based on fact and reason from ego involvement. They state, "In a negotiation, particularly in a bitter dispute, feelings may be more important than talk."[13] The authors emphasize that both sides almost always approach negotiation with strong feelings. The shrewd negotiator recognizes that the other side harbors such emotions and allows them to ventilate them without feeling threatened. Communication breaks down if both parties in the negotiation are trying to impress their followers and to trip up the other side. Success will come only when both parties look at issues and try to separate them as much as possible from the emotions which are strongly felt by the negotiators and their followers.

Take the example of the administrators and faculty who have dug in their heels over salary. The administration states it cannot go beyond a 4 percent raise and the faculty are just as vehement in saying they won't budge an iota below 6 percent. Rather than starting with that volatile and publicly proclaimed position, shrewd persuaders on either side would begin by getting agreement on something not nearly as explosive. They might agree on meeting times, location and length of the sessions. They would then tackle a relatively minor point about the school's insurance policy. From there, they would go on to get agreement about a small dispute—something like whether faculty can be paid on a 9, 10 or 12-month salary. From there, they would establish mutually agreed upon criteria. Such criteria might include: (1) any contract should be consistent with salary increases at comparable schools, (2) any increase should not decrease salaries for other groups within the school, such as secretarial staff, (3) any salary increase should be given within the boundaries of a balanced budget.

If both sides have agreed on a number of issues and have not felt put down or defeated, they're much more likely to get the crucial salary issue settled once it gets on the table. Such an approach is also called the "win-win" method because in the inevitable tussle of negotiations, all parties emerge with a sense of accomplishment and victory. And the key to the "win-win" approach has been the focus on the issues with a strong sensitivity for the feelings of the other side.

Summary of Key Points

1. The court system is one of the last arenas where logical arguments must be presented to win cases. While attorneys and judges can and do apply emotional appeal, a case must be grounded in arguments backed by solid evidence.

2. While trials are based on reason, a court case doesn't carry the same certainty as logic or math. Participants in a trial try to come as close as they can to the ideal of absolute truth and certainty but know they fall short. Therefore, they try to make their case as *probable* as they can to a jury or judge.

3. While emotional appeals seem to work best with many, sometimes they can backfire. Some listeners insist on "proof" and get turned off when it's not presented. They find the strongly emotional approach suspect and shallow. Successful persuaders, therefore, match their approach to the audience.

4. What may seem reasonable to one person may appear outlandish to the next. So, effective motivators probe the mind-set of their listeners and avoid promoting positions considered illogical by their audience.

5. Persuaders usually do better when they present both sides of a controversial issue. If they don't bring out and answer an objection hovering in the minds of an audience, the listeners will mentally refute them.

6. Many successful persuaders try to get an audience to focus on the issues rather than emotions, especially in a conflict situation. They avoid beginning with a publicly stated position because such positions involve pride and usually prolong the negotiations. They start by getting their opponents to agree on easy issues before they move to the tough ones.

5

Self-Motivation

Sally Clark is a nurse educator with a tough mission. In her smoking cessation classes, she works to get smokers to convince themselves to quit —no easy task for her or them. The people who sign up for Sally's course really want to kick a habit they know endangers their health and guarantees hostile glances from non-smokers. But how to do it when merely willing and wishing something isn't enough? A combination of chemical and psychological dependence makes giving up cigarettes one of the hardest things they'll ever do. They've all heard the gruesome statistics about emphysema and heart attacks. They've also endured countless sermonettes from well intentioned family and friends who have no clue about how hard it is to stop.

Smoking is just one example of a habit that's hard to break. Humans can get chained to almost anything—over-eating, sexual addiction or biting their fingernails. Have a Diet Pepsi or a Snickers at the same time every day and pretty soon you're hooked.

The Power of Habit

Habit is the key to self-persuasion. Habits are easy to fall into and hard to break. As a result, they're powerful motivators. Horace Mann described a habit as a series of threads which tie together daily to form a cable that is almost impossible to break. Most of us are not even aware of how we drift into any human habit, but once established, habits burrow into our psyches. And it doesn't make much difference whether the habit is bad or good, the same principle applies. If one person's diet is junk food, it's hard to start eating fruits and vegetables. Any time someone tries to break away, the body rebels. It says "Hey, I like twinkies, potato chips and beer. You have no right to take them away and if you do, I'll make you suffer with withdrawal symptoms." If someone else gets in the habit of daily exercise, she'll feel remorse if she can't workout.

Some human needs have to be satisfied but others don't. No one can get by without food, water and air. But there are other drives that become habitual only when they're reinforced through constant practice. While sex is a natural drive, humans are able to live productive lives without it if they so choose. They can also do without coffee, alcohol, junk food and cigarettes. But once they get hooked, what was formerly a pleasure becomes a near necessity.

Because the habit is a series of threads intertwined in a cable of steel, the cable has to be broken. Anyone who has either tried to cut a cable or break a strongly ingrained habit knows this is a big order. Being *willing* to change is not nearly enough. Successful self-motivators make it only if they start a new habit to replace the old one.

Smoking is one of the hardest habits to break because smokers are dealing with the double binding power of psychological addiction and chemical dependence. Like food, smoking is associated with more than physical pleasure. Just as a good meal satisfies hunger and brings back happy memories of dinner with a dear friend, smoking satisfies the nicotine craving but also provides other benefits to the smoker. It gives some smokers something to do with their hands. For others, the cigarette has become an integral part of the morning coffee break or the evening meal. Somehow, a special dinner isn't complete without dessert, coffee and a final smoke.

Sally Clark explains how cigarettes have become woven into the fabric of a smoker's life and then offers to help unravel the threads: "In my workshops, I encourage smokers to recognize the unconscious factors which trigger the urge to smoke. For most smokers, the cigarettes help them to relax, celebrate an accomplishment or concentrate on a task. But this response has become automatic and associated with other activities in their daily routine."

To succeed, the smoker who wants to quit must replace pleasant thoughts and emotions linked to the habit with equally pleasant and dominant thoughts and emotions that focus on the benefits of breaking the habit. A firm, abstract resolve with nothing to back it will melt like snow in the sun when positioned against years of vividly remembered pleasant experiences strongly linked to chemical addiciton. Join that to the rationalization of many smokers that they'll "gain weight" if they stop, and it's easier to see why abstract resolutions are doomed from the start. Smokers who stop for good are the ones who fuse resolve with methods that work. They know that simply giving themselves "good reasons" for their actions doesn't do it. They have to feel as strongly about their new habit as they did about the old one.

Smokers who succeed in stopping begin by branding in their mind the most vivid image they can muster. They focus not only on their resolve to quit, but also on the feeling of the self-satisfaction they know they'll experience once they've ingrained a new habit. Smokers, overeaters and the undisciplined—in other words 99 percent of the human race—will succeed only if they graft onto their psyche a new set of mental images and emotional feelings. They call up an all-out attack and enlist all of their senses in the battle. Self motivation signs are plastered on bathroom mirrors and apartment exits. Motivational cassettes are plugged into car stereos. Habit-breakers also seek out people like themselves who can offer support and encouragement when the going gets tough. Every time they're tempted to fall, they immediately call up the strongest image of why they're making a change in their lives.

As graphically as he can, the smoker pictures in his mind a new person free from smoker's breath and nicotine-stained fingers. He also knows he won't have to brace himself for the hostile glances of non-smokers every time he lights up in public. Instead of thinking how hard it is not to smoke, he focuses on the euphoria of knowing he did something really difficult and survived as a healthier and better person.

He doesn't dwell on the highly attractive ads depicting happy smokers because he knows they can rekindle his desire. If he has an occasional slip and lights up, he won't punish himself mentally, but will make a new resolve and move on. Any temporary failure will be seen as data for re-evaluating and improving his performance for the next time. He asks himself what he learned from this slippage so he can do better when temptation strikes again.

Self-Motivation and Sexual Addiction

If the urge to smoke is a problem only for smokers, the sexual drive affects virtually everyone who is human. Donald Joy, a professor of human development and Christian education, tells numerous stories of people who feel trapped by sexual addiction.[1] As a Christian theologian, Joy emphasizes that sex is a special form of union reserved for marriage and is a source of deep joy for husband and wife. The most fulfilling marriages are those in which sex is a unique expression of love. But he also discusses the problems millions of people have of confining sex to marriage. Many are shackled by the chains of pornography or fornication and desperately want to escape but don't know how. Like any other deeply entrenched habit, addiction to compulsive sex is hard to break.

Most agree with the psalmist that there is a time to embrace and a time to refrain from embracing. The challenge is to keep the sexual drive in line with moral principles. If someone has been sexually active but has decided for good reasons to be celibate, how does he tame a drive that has become a habit? It won't be done by a mere act of the will. As with any other strong force, an equally strong habit has to be put in its place.

When we Catholic teenagers were growing up in the 50s we heard plenty of sermons on "avoiding the near occasion of sin." Such a phrase wasn't completely clear, but we knew it had something to do with heavy necking or lingering glances at the pin-ups in *Esquire* magazine, the much milder version of *Playboy* in the fifties. Most of us endured an earnest teacher who ticked off a list of so-called near occasions of sin. But despite the stuffiness of the phrase, "near occasion of sin" is a valid principle. A distinction can be made between sin and the near occasion of sin. Someone can put himself in such a position that it's almost impossible not to succumb. Successful reformed alcoholics know they can't have that first drink. They also realize they can't roam the bars after work, stare at a glass of scotch on the counter and expect that this will somehow strengthen their resolve not to drink anymore.

If a man is trying to get over an addiction to pornography, it won't help to keep looking at *Playboys* and *Penthouses* with the hope that he won't become aroused. Experts on self-motivation emphasize that the first step is to admit there is an addiction, especially in regard to unbridled sex and drinking. The second is to avoid situations in which the addict gets blown away because the object of the compulsion is staring him in the face.

One of the worst forms of self-motivation is a grim determination to avoid an activity like unwanted sex or overeating and then to dwell on how tough it is to go without. That's like someone telling you "You must *not* think of chocolates"—a sure guarantee for seeing chocolates everywhere. Celibacy and self-discipline work best when they're seen as avenues to greater rewards.

Humans don't live in a vacuum. A bad habit has to be replaced by a good one. If it's not, the old habit will lift its head and temptation becomes obsession. That's why people who are trying to give up one form of addiction must replace it with something that is far more constructive. A mere resolve to stay celibate works only for the small percentage of highly disciplined humans. But motivated people who can transfer sexual energy into something creative not only solve their problem of addiction to sex, but also produce some other positive results in their lives.

Many artists realize that a period of celibacy frees them to develop other facets of their creativity and to focus their energies not on sex but on producing great paintings or poetry. Athletes will give up sex for a time to concentrate on their sport. For these people, celibacy or self-control is seen not so much as a negative act of avoiding temptation but as a re-channeling of energy into something productive. Artists and athletes concentrate more on the joys of their accomplishments gained through discipline than they do on how much they're giving up.

The person who wants to remain celibate, even for a short time, concentrates on the sense of being in control rather than the difficulty of doing without. In her book *The New Celibacy*, Gabrielle Brown cites a number of people who have become celibate for a time and find new joy in their lives as a result. Don, a 32-year-old store manager, states: "I noticed a kind of heightened perception in understanding people. I began to 'see' women as people, maybe for the first time. A funny thing was that women became inordinately attracted to me, perhaps because I gave them a certain kind of attention that was really more powerful than sexual attention."[2] Roxanne, a 54-year-old fashion coordinator, underscores the advantages of celibacy in her life: "For me, being celibate doesn't mean I'm blocking my sexuality. I use it and it keeps me strong, dynamic, youthful."[3] Successful celibates focus on the advantages of their chosen state and reinforce the positive aspects.

Commitment

The thread of commitment is woven through the accomplishments of virtually every achiever who has made a plan and stuck to it. Salespeople know that if they can get us to commit ourselves to anything—taking a test drive, accepting a small gift or even a brochure—they have a much better chance of convincing us to buy their product.

Super-achievers are particularly adept at applying this principle to themselves. In addition to conjuring vivid images of benefits they know they'll gain from their resolutions, they purposely commit themselves to an action to make sure it will be carried out.

Before I returned to graduate school, I knew my brother Dave had taken the Evelyn Wood Reading Dynamics program before he started Law School. He correctly believed that if he could increase his reading speed, he would do better in his law classes. I wanted to take the course myself but knew that it cost about $700 at the time. So I called a reading expert at my alma mater and asked the question: is it worth it for me to invest $700 in a speed reading course. He answered by saying "It depends on you. You can go down to any bookstore and find a manual on how to improve your reading skills. If you set up and follow a regular program, you'll accomplish what you want." I questioned further: "Then why don't most people do that?" He said, "Courses in almost any subject are based on the premise that people not only need the instruction, but also the commitment of time and money in order to keep themselves motivated. If we can psyche ourselves and stay that way, we could learn and save money in the process. If you know you can't keep with it, invest the money and the Tuesday evenings."

This same principle applies to almost any human accomplishment. Learning a language is possible with tapes and books, but not too many have the discipline and self-motivation to stick with a program that will make them fluent. Most of us need not only the instruction, but the jet-propulsion of commitment to persevere. The same is true of weight loss and body conditioning. It doesn't take a genius to figure out that humans almost always drop some pounds and tone muscles with a reduction in food and an increase in exercise. The difficult part comes from sticking with a regular program that will accomplish those two tasks.

A Realistic Plan

Self-motivation works best when it's carried out in small, purposeful chunks. People who set grandiose goals often fail simply because the mountain is too high. The old cliché "A journey of a thousand miles begins with a single step" applies to self-motivation. For a long time, I admired people who wrote books and resolved I would write one myself. I talked about it to friends and even jotted down an outline or two. But I was all talk and no action. Lurking in the back of my mind was the fear of rejection from editors. I had read about the "awful truth of the publishing business" that many authors *never* get published.

I had been an administrator for nine years and when I returned to full-time teaching, I resolved to start writing every day. But it was hard to get going. The phrase "Apathy, apathy everywhere—but I don't care" kept ringing in my brain. I felt good when I actually sat down and composed something but I wasn't doing it on a daily basis. I remembered a statement a former professor had made: "No one really enjoys writing, but everyone really enjoys having written something good." Spurred on by this thought, I resolved to write an hour a day. But unless I backed my resolve with a vivid image of why I was writing, the day would go by without a line on paper—or word processor. So, I began to focus on the positive feeling I would get when the hour was logged. Writing can be a lonely process and unless the writer imagines the rewards, it's hard to keep going.

I also read books about writers and tried to find out what made them go on day after day. Authors like the prolific Isaac Asimov intrigued me. In the introduction to his book on humor,[4] Asimov tells how much he dreaded vacations unless he could write. He writes over seven hours a day every day and assures his readers that he wouldn't want to do anything else. I couldn't understand why someone would like chaining himself to his writing desk all day and find it a pain to break away for a vacation. But once I started concentrating on the *benefits* of writing, I could see why many writers enjoy their craft. Such benefits include a feeling of satisfaction from creating thoughts and putting them on paper, the joy of a published article or book and positive reaction from readers. Motivated writers, like other self-motivators beam in on the advantages and pleasure of what they do and either eliminate or play down the disadvantages.

The beginning stages of habit change are the hardest, and strong motivational methods have to be applied at this stage. Successful self-motivators usually go through the following steps:

1. They make a strong resolution to change.

2. They then support this resolve with a vivid picture of *why* they want to break the habit.

3. Every time they're tempted to fall, they call up their original strong reasons for wanting to start the new habit.

4. They reinforce such reasons with vividly imagined benefits of taking on the new habit.

5. They also dwell on the bad features of the habit they want to break.

6. They go through this process every time they're tempted.

Single-Mindedness and Focusing

Last summer, my son Joel talked me into buying a cocker spaniel. I asked the seller for the most mellow pup in the litter and we brought home a dog that turned out to be anything but docile. We called him "Homer" and he has the usual disposition of cockers—feisty but affectionate. But he also carries in his genes another trait—Homer is single-minded. His current fetish is a stocking. Last month, he was into ripping newpapers. If we tried to hide the object of his desire or to distract him, Homer became even more determined. Put the sock behind the sofa and he'd do anything to squirm into that narrow space. Place it five shelves up the bookcase and he would stare at it with the look of someone who's willing to wait a long time.

Strong self-motivators are like that. They set their goals and then rivet their energies on that goal. If they're told they can't, they tell you they can. They've developed the habit of focusing on their goals and then doing whatever it takes to reach those goals.

Focusing is one of the hardest human skills to master. It's too easy to get constantly distracted and discouraged by the thousand daily events competing for attention. But focusing pays rich dividends in getting jobs done and staying sane in the process. Focused people are calm and productive because they've learned to block out anything they don't consider top priority. They're also more alert and less stressed because they concentrate on the important task at hand. They avoid what I call "mind-jamming." Mind-jamming is the effort to try to think two or three thoughts at once rather than focusing on what's most important at the moment. Mind-jamming happens when a nervous speaker goes blank during a talk—an experience enjoyed only by masochists. The orator is in the middle of a story and forgets his place. Panic. So what does he think about? The subject of his talk and the audience? He tries to but he's absorbed in the morass of realizing that he doesn't know where he is in the outline or manuscript. His mind is jammed with three thoughts—(1) I've gone blank and I'm not enjoying this, (2) where was I? and (3) all those people out there are waiting for me to keep talking.

If he focuses on the *topic* only, he'll almost certainly get quickly back on track and the audience won't even know that he's had a brief bout of amnesia. With a four to one ratio of thought speed to voice speed, he'll also gradually be able to notice the friendly faces in the audience and think about his subject. By focusing on what is most important, he saves the day and the speech.

Humans pay a high price for not focusing. Inattention costs millions of dollars every year in accidents and mistakes. Cars go off roads or crash into each other because one of the drivers was distracted. A million dollar deal is lost because a manager was preoccupied with something else. How many times have we missed key ideas in a meeting because our mind was 500 miles away? Employees who are supposed to be thinking about one project are distracted by another and neither gets done well. The divided mind is an easy trap and most of us fall into it on a regular basis. Successful self-motivators have become adept at single-mindedness.

Willpower

Focusing and single-mindedness are vital, but neither works without willpower. Humans are the only beings on this planet who have to join mind and will to get anything done. In explaining the importance of will, Plato uses the analogy of a chariot with two horses. One horse, the good, is willing to stay on the road and trot toward the destination, but the unruly horse, the bad, is always trying to go off to the side. "Will" is the driver who tries to keep the unruly horse on track. So it is with most of us. We can see we should do something and want to do it, but it's hard. St. Paul says: "I don't understand myself at all, for I really want to do what is right, but I can't. I do what I don't want to—what I hate."[5]

We might resolve to get better organized and to make better use of our time at work, but find that we give in to the same old distractions and before we know it, the morning is gone in a vapor cloud of inefficiency. Many a well-intentioned professional starts the work-day by writing down a list of to-do items and prioritizing them according to what should be done first. But let the first interruption strike, and he's off on a two-hour tangent. Before he knows it, he has spent seven minutes on project "A" and an hour and 45 minutes on tasks that are trivial. But some have honed their wills to concentrate on what they believe is most important and stay with it.

Winston Churchill had an iron will and used it, especially during crises. With bulldog tenacity, Churchill rallied the British to resist Hitler's pummeling during his nation's darkest hour. Churchill had severe stage fright. If he had to give a speech in Parliament, he spent the previous day in bed concentrating on what he would say. Like most effective speakers, he knew his best weapon for overcoming fear of speaking and the Nazis was to meet the fear head-on and to conquer it. There is a saying, "Do the thing you fear the most, and the death of fear is certain." But doing takes willpower and statesmen like Churchill dug down deep to accomplish what they wanted.

Perseverance and Accentuating the Positive

"He's the best salesman I have ever seen." These words were used by Tom Moore, a sales manager who was describing Ted Endicott. Endicott is special not merely because he sells 40 cars a month—almost twice as many as the top salespeople in this country—but because he is also blind. In 1983, Ted Endicott heard the news from doctors that he had contracted a fungal disease called histoplasmosis.

Out of a job and sightless, he travelled to numerous dealerships trying to get someone to give him the chance to sell. Finally, sales manager Tom

Blanco decided to hire him over the phone, because Endicott exuded such confidence. Thousands of salespeople with eyes to see and months of training have given up because they weren't self-motivated enough to persevere, especially when the going got rough. Endicott attributes his success to hard work and help from his wife Ann and fellow workers. But two other factors account for his success as America's top salesman in 1987. Ted Endicott motivates himself on a daily basis and he accentuates his positive features while playing down the negative ones. He says that most of his customers aren't aware that he's blind. He has completely memorized the car lot. "I never tell anyone I can't see. I sell cars because I am a good salesman, not because I am blind."[6]

Strong self-motivators concentrate on what they do well and keep building on their strengths. They're aware of but not dominated by their handicaps. Like Ted Endicott, they use a handicap as a spur to succeed where others have failed. Crises are seen as challenges and each victory is a stepping stone to the next success. Self-motivators take pride in meeting the difficult, beating it and getting better in the bargain. Negative images and destructive self-talk are banished and replaced with a steady conversation that they can overcome obstacles. They enjoy the satisfaction of knowing they have met the enemy of discouragement and won.

Pessimistic salespeople focus on the rejection and the feeling of losing out on another sale. They then apply this thought to their entire life and see themselves as failures not merely in their chosen profession of sales, but in virtually everything else they do. The old adage that an optimist sees the glass as half full and a pessimist sees it as half empty applies to self-motivation. Hamlet's comment in Act II of Shakespeare's play is close to the truth: "There is nothing either good or bad, but thinking makes it so." Strong self-motivators know that they are, to a large degree, what they think they are. And what they think they are is molded by the thoughts they put into their minds.

Commitment, Benefits and Habit

I have long believed that an early morning meditation period is a great motivator. I learned the method when I was a Jesuit seminarian and we had to go through a 45-minute meditation at 5:30 in the morning. When I first started, I found it hard to bounce out of bed and sit for 45 minutes praying and applying some scriptural reading to my life. But after awhile, the habit became so ingrained that I have continued to do a shorter version ever since.

Meditating not only provides a way to soothe the mind and cleanse the spirit, but it can be a powerful form of self-motivation. If humans are propelled by the thoughts placed in their mind, meditation provides a vehicle for planting those thoughts that best motivate. When I teach workshops on rebuilding a postitive self image or reducing stress, I strongly advocate a five to 15-minute mediation period each day. Some people are "larks" and they like to meditate in the morning. Others are "night owls" and the evening is their best time. But the key to making the method work is to do it every day at the same time.

Successful self-motivators find that meditation followed by guided imagery gives them a double edge: they start the day relaxed and they rehearse events before they happen. I like to begin with a scriptural passage and concentrate on it for a few minutes. I might take Proverbs 3:27 "Withhold not good to whom it is due, when it is in the power of thine hand to do it."[7] I dwell on that passage and then relate it to the day ahead. As a teacher, parent or friend, I try to apply the advice.

The next step is to vividly imagine oneself applying the thought to the coming day. I not only think, "I owe it to my students to be well prepared," but as vividly as possible, I imagine myself spending time reading, going over notes and then walking into the classroom to give the lecture.

Inner Visions

She was 19 when she died but she accomplished more in her life than most teenagers. Her name was Joan of Arc and she stands not only as a symbol of fierce determination and integrity but as a woman strongly propelled by her own self-motivation. When she was 14 years old, Joan heard voices and saw a blaze of light. [8] Fearing her peasant father's disapproval, she kept the voices and images to herself though they continued over the next two years. Gradually both voices and visual images turned out to be St. Michael, St. Catherine of Alexandria and St. Margaret. The three saints instructed Joan, a peasant girl, to save France by leading the French soldiers against the English who occupied her country.

In 1428, Joan's inner voices compelled her to go to a French commander by the name of Robert de Baudricourt to announce that she was divinely chosen to lead the French against the English. Skeptical at first, French officials finally agreed out of desperation because their forces were losing the war.

Equipped with a small army and dressed in white armor, Joan rallied her soldiers through the English lines near Orleans and captured an English fort. She then went on to a second victory at Patay.

In the third battle near Paris, Joan was wounded and spent the winter recuperating. In the spring of 1430, she led a group of French soldiers against the English but this time, through a blunder on the part of the French governor, she and her soldiers were defeated. Joan was taken prisoner, put in a tower and turned over to the English. To save face, the enemy could not execute her because she had beaten them in battle, but they could and did try her for witchcraft and heresy. In 1431, she was brought before the court of the Inquisition. Here, she was grilled about her visions, her wearing of male attire and her commitment to the Church.

At the end of the first trial, the judges called Joan a heretic and an agent of the devil. The tribunal handed her over to the local government for public burning unless she confessed that she was a witch and that she had lied about her inner voices. While her fear of the flames caused her to confess once that her inner voices were false, she reasserted that what she was hearing was divinely inspired. She was then led out to be burned. As the flames flickered up her legs and touched her face, she riveted her eyes on a cross held by a Dominican monk and called out the name of Jesus. Immediately after she died, bystanders cried out, "We're lost; we've burned a saint." Twenty-five years later after the English had been defeated, Joan's case was reheard posthumously. This time she was vindicated and in 1919 was canonized in the Catholic Church.

Joan of Arc exemplifies the power of self-persuasion. Whether her voices were real or vividly imagined, her inner perception motivated her to do something that in retrospect seems astounding. For Joan, the visions were vivid and unrelenting. Without the vision, she would have stayed an obscure peasant girl and no one would have known about her. But she demonstrates that persuasion is primarily what goes on in each individual's mind.

Strong self-motivators fix in their minds a vivid image and hold it in place until they accomplish their goals. Visionaries are people who know what they want, keep that image strong and then pursue it with passion. They don't live in the world of vague abstractions. For Joan of Arc, her vision was the need to rescue France and do what she thought God wanted. For Martin Luther King, the inner vision was a land where black children would have all the rights of whites. King's inner vision was proclaimed outwardly in his "I Have a Dream" speech. For Mitch Snyder of Washington, D.C., the inner vision was one of the homeless finding their basic needs. All three have one element in common: they grafted a picture in their minds of what they wanted and kept the image there. Theirs was not a world of gray but one of vivid colors.

Summary of Key Points

1. Deeply embedded habits like smoking or sexual addiction are difficult to stop. Therefore, people who want to motivate themselves to change a habit need a specific program.

2. Such a program consists of vividly imagining the benefits received from a change of habit and then constantly focusing on those benefits, especially when one is tempted to revert to the old habit.

3. Self-motivators need to be aware of the "triggers" which tempt them. For a smoker, the trigger might be a coffee break or a festive dinner. For someone addicted to sexual pleasure, the trigger might be pornography.

4. The new habit must be repeated enough times so that it takes the place of the old one. Daily meditation and vividly imagined benefits are two steps in this direction.

5. Successful self-motivators constantly keep their inner vision in mind and the vision becomes a constant source of self-persuasion.

6

Protection from Persuasion: Knowing When and How to Resist Advertising and Sales

On Saturday morning, they sit mesmerized by the cartoons and conned by the commercials. Advertisers sometimes refer to them as "consumer trainees" rather than children and they're learning early allegiances to products which promise them happiness.[1] If we've ever joined our children on a Saturday morning and watched the televised parade of cartoons, we know the power they have in keeping us entertained. But we pay a high price for this habit. For unmatched pressure, bring a four-year-old shopping right after the cartoons. Earnest, high-pitched voices cajole parental victims into buying whatever cereal was promoted that morning on the tube. If we go within ten miles of a toy store, we're nudged into "just going in to look" at the latest Masters of the Universe or G.I. Joe complete sets. Before the day is over, we've spent more on groceries than we planned and despite our best efforts to resist, have bought yet another toy to add to a collection which is larger than many small town Toys 'R Us stores.

Adults are not much better at resisting the siren song of the advertisers. Despite our efforts to live within a budget, our bloated credit cards offer nagging testimony that we often spend more than we should. We're like the Greek hero Odysseus in Homer's *The Odyssey*. In the ancient story, sailors were often lured to their death by the sweet songs of the sirens who beckoned from the shore. So powerful was their melodic plea that any ship traveling through the straits would veer to the right after the sailors heard the harmonies.

Odysseus knew that navigators before him had been too smug about their ability to hear the songs and not be seduced by the sweet but fatal harmonies. So he had his sailors put wax in their ears. He then instructed his crew to tie him to the mast and told them that, under no circumstances, should he be released until the ship had passed through the narrow channel. He emphasized that his men should disregard any orders he gave while the music was playing.

We're often like Odysseus, because despite our attempts to resist, we succumb to the influence of the ads. This should not be surprising because the advertisers are skilled in promoting their products. In a democratic society, our only protection is to recognize the tactics and then make buying decisions based on sound judgement rather than impulse. Odysseus made it through the straits because he had a plan. Like Odysseus, we need some practical methods for resisting persuasion when it doesn't really make our life better.

A Good Word About Advertising

It would be too easy to blast advertisers as con artists trying to sell their wares without concern for the consumer. Such is not my intention, because I firmly believe in the value of advertising for fueling the economy. Besides, television, radio, newspaper and magazine ads are highly entertaining. Some are far more interesting than the programs they sponsor. Commercials have become embedded in our North American culture. They both embody and reflect our way of life. Without them, we would have to pay for all of our televised football games, news programs and fine dramatic productions.

But if we don't know the techniques of the professional advertisers, we're far more vulnerable to buying on impulse. Many of the decisions we make are a direct result of strong emotional appeal rather than careful consideration and prudent buying habits.

A few years ago, an ad appeared in a newspaper and promised a "sure cure for cockroaches." Readers were asked to send in $10. For anyone who bit, a package arrived about two weeks later with two small blocks. Instructions read: "Place the cockroach on block A and smash it with block B." That is false advertising and is not the subject of this chapter. If few ads are false, many are irrational.

Why the Emotional Appeal?

It's hard to blame advertisers for the emotionally oriented ads which dominate the media. Advertisers respond to what the public wants and what they believe works best. Companies have tried the rational approach, but have found that it usually fizzles. Try to imagine a commercial featuring a no-nonsense type of announcer who begins by presenting three good reasons why we should buy Pepsi. The ad would go something like this: "There are three major reasons why you should buy Pepsi: (1) it quenches thirst, (2) it's reasonably priced and (3) we need your money. No, the ad opens with happy, athletically thin and exuberant 28-year-olds scampering on a beach. They're drinking Diet Pepsi and they're feeling good. And even though you're now eligible to join AARP (the Association of American Retired Persons), you too can be part of the Pepsi generation by drinking from this carbonated fountain of youth.

When we watch and analyze most ads, we notice a curious phenomenon. Many of them are not merely directed at the emotions—they're illogical. Take the one about the handsome soap opera actor whose face exudes sincerity as he tells us, "I'm not a doctor, but I play one on TV." After this self-confession, he then dispenses medical advice about what pain-reliever we should use. And what about the aspirin commercial featuring a thousand doctors stranded on a desert island who would choose Bayer over any other aspirin? The *New Yorker* featured a Charles Adam's cartoon showing an ad man standing in a row boat with a bullhorn. His question was directed to a thousand doctors standing together on a tiny desert island: "All right. Now, how many would prefer Bayer?"

The Irrational Ads: Why Do We Succumb?

How did we come to the point of being lured by commercials which don't make sense? Shortly after World War II, Austrian psychologist Ernest Dichter came to the United States and established the Institute for Motivational Research. Using a Freudian approach, Dichter focused on what worked in advertising and what didn't. For example, Dichter concluded that Chrysler sold more sedans than convertibles because men regarded a sedan as a wife and a convertible as a mistress. Other experts like Herta Herzog focused on power as a strong need for buying products.[2] The advocates of Motivational Research emphasized that often consumers make decisions based more on irrational needs than on sound judgment. Take, for example, the now classic Marlboro ad which features a rugged cowboy with the creased face riding the range and smoking America's most masculine cigarette. Back in the fifties, the Phillip Morris Co. wanted to promote Marlboro, a filter cigarette, but knew that many smokers perceived the filter as "effeminate."[3]

At the time, western programs were popular on television. So a campaign was launched to reassure men that filters were masculine. The first ads depicted a rugged, Telly Savalas type who looked tough and pensive. On his right hand was a small tattoo—a sure sign he had been in and out of a few ports. But our hero was not simply a rough cowboy who rode the range. He was probably a busy executive who worked during the week and then rode horses on his rustic ranch someplace in the hills. He was the consummate all-American Renaissance man who combined intelligence, western ruggedness and masculinity into one leathery package.

How many men would wake up one morning and say to themselves: "My masculinity has been taking a beating lately. But if I smoke Marlboros, I can feel manly again." Logic gives way to the irrational.

Logic and beer don't necessarily mix, but consider the success of the beer commercials in gaining and keeping the allegiance of loyal brew consumers. Some can get downright passionate about which beer they prefer and switching brands would be a little less honorable than selling your three year old at a garage sale. The two top beers in the United States are Miller and Budweiser. There's also a certain mystique about German beers like Heineken and Lowenbrau. But in an informal study, ABC correspondent John Stossel found that beer drinkers couldn't really pick their favorite brands in a taste test.[4] In fact, the least advertised beer was Shaffers. The serious and willing sippers preferred it over Bud and Miller when the beers were offered without being identified by brand.

If dedicated beer drinkers are asked why they choose one brand over another, they usually respond by saying they buy for taste. But a few will admit that packaging and the ads are the real motivators. Miller conjures up a myriad of tough but likeable helicopter pilots, stevedores, professional and weekend athletes—the kind of guys who quaff Miller after a rough-and-tumble game or job.

Fighting Back

There are a number of ways to counter the illogic of many ads. One is to examine the validity of the claims being made. Rather than getting swept into the vortex of the strong emotional/irrational appeals, we can take a hard look at whether the products provide a genuine service or simply try to get consumers to buy more than they need. I have to admit liking those ads which confirm that I've made a sound decision in buying something I really need like basic transportation, insurance, medical care or food. What I don't like are promotions aimed at getting me to buy on impulse for no good reason.

Everyone likes a bargain and Americans in particular are on the look-out for a good deal. If we want a sure-fire way to save money, we should follow this simple guideline: when we have a choice between two products of comparable quality, buy the one that is *least* advertised. Why? Quite simply, it will almost always cost less. Major manufacturers may be providing services, but their bottom line is to make a profit. When they invest heavily in advertising, they normally pass the cost on to the consumer. Try this experiment. Next time you tour the medicine section of the supermarket or drugstore, compare the cost of Bayer per pill with a little advertised brand like Norwich. In many cases, the price doubles or triples.

So why do we fall for this enormous cost hike? Because the sincere man in the trench coat or the actor walking the beaches of the desert island tells us that only Bayer is pure aspirin. Think about it, though. Are the other aspirins a combination of aspirin and peanut butter? Do they use impure ingredients? No, they don't advertise as much. And that's why the price is lower. Aspirin is aspirin. Bayer is a fine product, but so are others which aren't advertised.

While there are some exceptions to this guideline of buying the less promoted product, it applies in most cases. Test it for cereals, soap, clothes, auto parts—or virtually any merchandise. What we're buying when we pick up the highly advertised item is some small emotional security because we're reinforced to believe that Bayer really will get rid of our headache faster or that we'll feel younger when we're drinking Diet-Pepsi. If we know what's happening to us, fine. But so often, we believe automatically that the most advertised goods are the best. But often, that's not true. As a result, we spend a lot of money to support the ads.

Living with Guilt

Appeal to guilt is another clever ploy for getting us to buy. How many have been reduced to a state of remorse because of the lonely and patient lady sitting by the phone, presumably for hours, waiting for us to reach out and touch her? This dear soul with the sweet, pained look *is our mother* who has spent years sacrificing herself for a hardened ingrate. Only the most insensitive jerk or calloused criminal would fail to call his mother.

The late Lorne Greene was one of television's most popular actors as he led the fight for truth, justice and well mannered adult sons on "Bonanza."

He also laid a guilt-trip on many dog owners for not feeding their beloved canine companions meat-enriched Alpo. By implication, owners who refused to give their dogs Alpo were only slightly less despicable than those who didn't call their mothers.

One of the most successful slogans of the last few years has been Hallmark's "When you care enough to send the very best." Many a greeting card purchaser has paused at the card display before buying another brand. Getting a card other than Hallmark could mean you really don't care that much for the recipient. If you did, you would buy the very best. But who makes the claim that Hallmark is the best? Are all Hallmark cards really the very best?

Fear

In American Express commercials, Karl Malden plays on the fear of either going abroad without travelers checks, or even worse, buying an inferior brand—which includes everything else. We've seen the spots many times because American Express advertises so much. The young, middle-aged or retired couple are happily touring Hong Kong or Istanbul, when one of them realizes with a jolt that their money has disappeared. But twenty yards away is a kindly tour guide with an almost indecipherable accent who assures them that there's an American Express office right around the corner. But then the moment of horror. The wife replies with the words of improvident travelers worldwide: "But they weren't American Express." With a look hovering somewhere between profound pity and barely concealed contempt, the guide says "I'm sorry. I can't help you." Play this one out logically. Is American Express the only company with offices in other countries? Is the couple doomed to walk the streets of Calcutta with no money and no way to find another travelers check company?

The Sale Trap

One of the most magical words in advertising is "sale." While it's true that we can save money by watching and taking advantage of the sales, we often get hoodwinked into assuming that sale items are always cheaper. I knew a manager in my hometown who used a simple trick. When an item, like neatly stacked nylons, was not moving at $2.98 a pair, he would throw all the stockings into a disheveled pile with a sign stuck in the middle reading: "Today only, two pairs of nylons—$6.95." His method was a quick way to clear the table.

Another popular and effective sale is the "Going out of Business" spectacular. There was a jewelry store in the same town that was able to drag out such a sale for several years before wary customers caught on. Sales are extremely popular because not only do consumers get reduced prices but they gain the satisfaction of bragging to friends that they bought something "on sale," thereby reinforcing that they're smart buyers, which in turn, confirms a need to think about themselves as shrewd.

From Advertising to Sales

Media ads prepare the soil for the salesperson to plant the seed and gather the harvest. Like advertising, sales produce some very positive effects. But salesmanship has a downside, because a relatively small number of unscrupulous practitioners have given the profession a bad name. In Woody Allen's comedy *Take The Money and Run*, an incompetent thief named Virgil is caught and sent to prison. Because he misbehaves, Virgil is inflicted with one of the most severe tortures known to the incarcerated: he's locked for three days and nights in the same room with an insurance salesman.

Such a stereotype is unfair to the millions who perform a valuable service by selling with skill and integrity. People need housing, transportation and insurance. Legions of salespeople work according to the highest standards and genuinely like their customers. These professionals are honest and care about the quality of their products and the good of their clients. They enjoy making a living through selling, but they find greater satisfaction in serving people well. But there are charlatans who aren't honest and who care more about profit than service. These high-pressure, do anything-to-make-a-buck types cast a pall on the entire profession. Their tactics need close watching.

Tricks of the Unscrupulous

Fred and Marlene are newlyweds who need a car. They both work but their budget is tight so they decide in advance of a shopping trip what they can afford. As they walk into the gleaming automobile showroom, they're greeted by a smiling, sincere man in a checkered sports coat. He introduces himself as Mark and surprisingly doesn't talk about selling cars. He compliments the bride on her new outfit and starts asking questions. He's delighted to know that they're starting their life together as man and wife and wishes them all the best. Delicately, he steers the conversation around to the purpose of their visit. Learning that they are interested in buying a low cost, reliable and attractive car, he asks more questions. He finds out that the couple *prefer* something out of their price range but they realize they have to be *practical*. Mark assures them that maybe, just maybe, they can have the car they want at a reasonable price, so he glides them over to a shiny model which is beyond their budget but which is obviously their first choice. He smiles and then purrs: "Why don't we take a test drive—no obligation, no pressure."

The couple have some reservations about even stepping into this beauty for fear of getting hooked, but Mark has become their friend by now and it would appear rude to turn him down. Besides, what harm can come from a simple test drive? They can always say "no" and then look at the practical, within-budget, small station wagon when they're through with the test drive. So off they go with Marlene at the wheel, Fred fiddling with the stereo in the passenger side and their ally Mark beaming from the plush backseat. If they make remarks about the comfort and luxury of the upholstery, Mark echoes and reinforces their sentiments. If they say they really shouldn't be doing this because they might get attached to the car, he reassures them that "Hey, we're just taking a ride. No harm in that."

They cruise along the freeway and then wind through their neighborhood with quick waves to neighbors and friends. Their desire for this car is getting stronger. Who wants to drive a practical but dull, small station wagon when they're still young and could be the exuberant owners of this automotive masterpiece? The salesman senses that they're getting more and more locked into wanting the fancier model and primes himself to pounce. But when they get back to the showroom and reality, Fred asks the inevitable question: how much will this cost? They can really afford no more than $150 per month in payments. Mark then starts tapping out a quick series of figures on his calculator. With the same reassuring smile, the advocate/friend says, "Well, ordinarily your car—the one you really want—would be $240 per month, but I think I can get the boss to lower the price so your payments would come in at around $180—only $30 over your budget. Would that work for you?" After some fast figuring, the couple says, "If you can get it for that, go for it."

With a shrug and a "Say a prayer that I can convince him," our sales hero heads off to the glass enclosed office of his manager. Fred and Marlene nervously watch a pantomime unfold behind the glass as the two combatants duel with each other. They see Mark gesturing dramatically as he obviously tries to convince his boss that this couple deserves a break and that the price ought to be drastically lowered just for them. After five minutes, he returns, with a frown on his face, to announce that "He wouldn't go for the $180 a month on a 60-month contract, but I was able to get him down to $210. Is there any way you can fit that into your budget, especially since you like the car so much?" By this time, the hooked couple emit a small groan, but say in unison, "Let's do it. We can find the money someplace."

These folks have just gone through the sales tactic known as "low-balling." Like the sailors before Odysseus, they heard the music and found it irresistible. By the time their advocate marched off presumably to use his persuasive skills on the boss, they were teetering near the edge of commitment. They not only loved the car, but they liked the salesman. Mark was on their side and had spent so much time with them. To turn him down after all that work would create a guilt they couldn't endure. So they drove away with a new car and a five-year obligation to pay $60 per month over what they had decided they could afford.

Certainly, negotiation over a car is expected since virtually no one pays the sticker price. Every day, salespeople joust with their managers over price. But some deliberately use "low-balling" as a normal tactic to land a higher commission. They know in advance that they'll never be able to convince their manager to come down to the quoted figure, but they also realize that they have the power to create such a strong desire for a product, that unwary customers will ultimately agree to any price just short of outrageous.

Another tactic is the "there's another couple interested in this car, house or set of furniture (mark off your choice), and I don't want you to lose it." The huckster plays on the customer's fear that he's about to see someone else get the item he really wants. This approach utilizes the pressure tactic of making the customer believe that if he doesn't act now, the desired object will be gone and that there is only *one* like it in the *universe*. Buy it now or lose it forever.

The "bait and switch" approach brings legions of potential buyers to car lots and department stores all over the world. The ploy begins with an ad for a quality product at a seemingly low price. Automobiles are probably the most common example. Let's say we're tired of a car that has to be repaired once a month and breaks down 19 miles from any form of human life or auto repair. After a night of cursing the constant repair bills and unreliability of a car turned clunker, we notice an ad that shouts "Brand new Flambeau—only $99 per month." ("Brand" before "new" works a special magic.) Hey, we can fit that into the old family budget, even though the two youngest children will have to go without lunches for awhile. So, off we go to the dealership. When we arrive, the gracious salesman greets us and hears our request to see the car for only $99 per month. He then leads us to the most stripped-down model in the history of automotive engineering. We're talking basic transportation here with engine, wheels and body the only non-options.

If we want a few extras like upholstery, heat and a rearview mirror, the price starts climbing. Throw in dealer-preparation, transportation charges from the west coast docks, tax and license and the price soars. The preceding is exaggerated, but test it for yourself by writing down the price printed in the newspaper and the real cost once you reach the showroom.

As consumers, we often buy products we don't need or pay more than we should because we've been conned. I admit to succumbing to sales tactics, even though I teach and study the art of persuasion. But I also know that the best protection I have is to know the tactics and try not to keep falling for the same ploys. The phrase *Caveat emptor* was coined during Roman times, but is even more important today because sales has become such a sophisticated art. Salespeople receive months of training in how to read customers, create desire, head off and answer objections and close the deal. Consumers are often at a disadvantage because they don't know sales methods and consequently fall prey to the few charlatans who use shady tactics. The best salespeople are usually honest and concerned about customers because, in the long run, they know that those two qualities will bring return business. Besides, they also realize that performing a service through sales creates greater job satisfaction than making a few dishonest bucks.

Sales Protection

Even if a salesperson is completely honest and avoids some of the shady tactics of his seedier colleagues, we can still benefit by practicing some persuasion methods of our own. Not to protect ourselves from the polished skills of a seasoned professional is a sure way to make some poor judgements and spend more money than we had planned. We should know the steps ourselves.

Sales usually involves a three-part process of opening, middle and close. While there are hundreds of variations on these phases, each step has a definite purpose as a customer is led down the path to commitment.

Skilled professionals know that the way *not* to sell is to walk up to a customer and say "Hi, may I help you?" That opener gets an almost automatic "No, I'm just looking" response. Effective sellers first establish rapport and gain confidence. Joe Girard, one of the top car salesmen in the United States, uses a number of different openings, but he does what he needs to start the bonding process so essential to success. If someone comments on his shirt, he will literally offer it to the potential customer.[5] The salesperson exudes warmth and concern as he tries to accomplish two tasks during the opening. He wants to be our friend and knowledgeable expert on the product and he needs to "read" us so he can plan his strategy. What we wear, how we look, and what questions we ask all provide clues to our buying habits and our vulnerabilities.

The best salespeople will work with the information we provide. If we're shopping for a dependable, medium-sized microwave oven, the salesperson marches us over to the items that fit that description. But most trained professionals will at least try to sell the model that will yield the biggest profit and commission. And that's fair enough since they depend on such attempts to make a living. But often we don't need the bells and whistles that come with the more expensive models. Good salespeople will quickly sense when they should back off. The amateurs will keep pushing, often to the point of the complete turn-off.

During the middle part of the sales transaction, the expert tries two more approaches: (1) matching the product to the needs presented by the customer and (2) emphasizing the features. If the salesperson has done her job well and listened carefully, she'll work with what the customer has given her. Then, she'll emphasize what she sees as customer needs. If I'm on a fast-paced schedule and don't have much time to cook in a conventional oven, my sales consultant will emphasize the time-saving features of the microwave that best fit my situation.

Now comes crunch time. Salesperson and customer have gone through the tribal dance of opening and middle, but the most important phase for both is the close. This is the pay-off for the salesperson because she can't make a living unless she does well here. And many customers have been backed into an inescapable corner because they didn't know how to wriggle out of a bad deal. During this crucial segment, the experienced salesperson will be on the lookout for any objections voiced by the customer. The pro looks for and relishes such revelations because objections provide the clue for the answer that will close the sale. If I'm trying to sell you something and I don't know what's keeping you from buying, I'm at a distinct disadvantage. If you tell me it's price or the wrong color, I can adjust quickly.

Two dynamics are operating during the close. The customer is feeling anxious, especially about an expensive product like a car or quality piece of furniture. Torn by conflicting desires of wanting the beautiful three-piece bedroom set and the realization of how much it's going to cost over the next two years, the customer hesitates. The salesperson senses this and consequently will use the close which she thinks will work best. She may come right out and ask what's keeping us from "initialing the agreement." (No one "signs contracts" anymore because they appear too binding.) If we moan that we just finished paying off a large Visa card and don't want to get locked into more endless payments, she may recommend a 90-day, no interest plan. If that suggestion gets a frown, she may return to an emphasis on how much we like the quality of the oak in the furniture and claim that we'll never again get the pieces at the sale prices offered today. She may stress that if we wait until we've saved enough money, either this set will be gone or prices will increase by at least 30 percent. If she's good, she won't keep talking—she'll simply look at us with that reassuring friendly smile that says, "Hey, I'm your friend trying to do you a favor; helping you save some money and get what you obviously love."

Counter-Reactions

I like working with skilled salespeople because they're good at reading me and adapting to my needs. It's the amateurs who blunder along and push when they should back off. But even with the best sellers, I need some devices of my own to keep me from making bad decisions or spending more than I planned.

Step one is to know the tactics and to be aware of how they're being used. As a basic rule, the more expensive the product being sold, the better trained the salesperson. There are exceptions to this rule, but it holds in most cases. Sellers of insurance, houses, cars, expensive clothes and stocks are usually well trained and adept at using the many tactics emphasized in sales training programs.

So, if the buyer wants self-protection, she should decide in advance the item she wants and roughly how much she will pay for it. Studies confirm that the undecided consumer is the easiest mark for the successful salesperson. If we float into a store with the vague notion of perhaps buying a new stereo and we come face to face with a proficient seller, we're already three runs behind. Like Odysseus, we need an advance plan.

The customer can also utilize some of the same strategies during the opening, middle and closing segments of the transaction, since the seller is also susceptible to persuasion tactics. Begin with a warm, friendly "hello" and a clear description of what you want. Various openings could include, "I'm looking for a dependable, used car and I can't go beyond $4,000." Or, "I want insurance that will give me the highest protection at the lowest cost so I'm looking at your company and about three others." If the salesperson is reputable and honest, he'll work with you to get what you want. If he's not, he may start applying pressure and use whatever strategies are needed to close the sale. An auto salesperson might say, "If we can get you into this model and keep your payments the same as they are now, would you buy this car?" Your response could be, "You and I know that there is no way I can buy this new car and keep my payments the same as the three-year-old model I'm driving now."

The ultimate weapon in the sales transaction is the willingness to say no and walk away. Many customers have bought an item primarily because they feel so obligated to the seller. They say to themselves, "That nice person has spent all this time with me and has worked so hard, I can't say no. Besides, I want the new suit anyway, even though it's way over what I decided I could spend."

One of the best guides for products is *Consumer Reports*. This monthly watch-dog provides an objective and independent evaluation of items, from washing machines to computers. The magazine also lists the medium price range so the buyer has a good idea of whether he's being gouged. *Consumer Reports* does not accept advertising and thus is free to describe the good and bad features of products. The annual subscription price is a good bargain because regular reading can save so much money over a year. Consumers also get a better idea of quality merchandise and the price they're paying for it.

Summary of Key Points

1. Advertisers most often use an emotional rather than a logical appeal because it works better. Consumers are wise to carefully consider whether they really need a product or whether, like Odysseus, they're being serenaded by the sirens of advertising.

2. The more a product is advertised, the higher the price because the cost is almost always passed on to consumers. Consequently, consumers can save by buying the less promoted of two comparable products if the quality is the same.

3. In addition to the highly charged, emotional appeal, many of the ads are irrational and thus bear continuous monitoring.

4. While the majority of salespeople are honest and care about the customer, some aren't. Such types will resort to tactics like "low-balling" or "bait and switch" to get customers psyched and more vulnerable to high pressure tactics.

5. Even with highly reputable professionals, the consumer is at a disadvantage because the salesperson is a trained persuader. Consequently, customers need to be aware of and use tactics of their own either to resist or to get the most value for their money.

6. Say no if the product isn't right and don't feel guilty about it.

7

Contending with the Cults

"It was easy to get involved," said the 24-year-old woman with two small children. Her name was Liz and she was bored and lonely. One day, Liz was intrigued by a poster she noticed in a laundromat. The poster beckoned her to a seminar which promised to enrich her life. Liz coaxed her husband into going with her. He was quickly disenchanted, but she was impressed with the friendliness of the happy people there who seemed so sure they had found the meaning of life and the secret of happiness.

Soon Liz was joining her new friends for weekly study groups. She watched video tapes of an attractive and persuasive 47-year-old woman who claimed to be the "one, present messenger of God's voice on earth."[1] Liz soon learned how to "decree," a process of rapidly reciting complicated chants. Although she found decreeing difficult at first, she later came to look forward to the ritual as the best part of her day. The experience gave her a drug-like high and began to provide a sense of purpose to her life.

After five months, the Navy transferred her husband, a sailor, to the East and she stopped decreeing. Liz also started dancing again and took an occasional drink—two pleasures forbidden by the church. But even from a continent away, the group still had her under their spell. After giving birth to her first baby, she followed the church's precept that only parents should hold their infants for the first three months. This did not sit well with friends who wanted to snuggle and hug her new daughter.

The couple moved back to the Pacific Northwest after the husband's discharge from the military. He became quickly involved in a new job and school: she started feeling lonely again. At that point, Liz became re-involved with the church again. She resumed her habit of decreeing and began listening to audio tapes of the church's doctrines. Nine months later, the couple separated and Liz coped by getting immersed in the church.

Liz's mother and sister noticed strange behavior changes. She told them both to stop watching television and she became so upset one night at a family dinner that she ran out of a restaurant because she didn't approve of what she considered the sensuous background music. Finally, Liz decided she would go to Los Angeles to join the church's main group. The planned move prompted her family to hire deprogramming specialists who whisked her to a secret place in the Midwest. Here, the deprogrammers subjected her to an intense three days of counter-persuasion methods. Later, she went to a halfway house where she continued to attend workshops on understanding tactics used by cults. The whole deprogramming process cost Liz's mother $20,000, but she said it was worth it because she regained her daughter.

What Makes a Cult?

In some ways, cults are like mainline churches, with their emphasis on morality and the pursuit of a better life. But officials of the Cult Awareness Center in Coeur d'Alene, Idaho, insist that cults are different primarily in the way they persuade.[2]

The northern panhandle of Idaho is one of the most scenic and relatively isolated havens in the world and consequently the area has attracted a swarm of cults. The Cult Awareness Center in Coeur d'Alene was founded to alert the public about cult tactics and to help ex-members go through the often traumatic process of re-entering a world that has been foreign to them for months or years. The Center has published a list of those organizations which it considers cults. They include the Unification Church, the Church of Scientology, The Socialist Nationalist Aryan People's Party, and the Church Universal and Triumphant. The Center applies the term "cult" to a group not because of its theology but because of its behavior and tactics for recruiting and keeping members.

The Awareness Center labels cults destructive if they use mind control, exclude all outside messages and insist on total dedication to the organization. Certain motivational methods of the cults are not that different from traditional religious orders or military organizations. Anyone who has joined the Army or entered a seminary or convent has gone through an experience something like the indoctrination process used by cults. Recruits and novices are isolated from the world and receive a steady diet of information designed to train them in ways of the military group or religious organization. But the essential difference is the intensity of the persuasive methods and the dominance of a charismatic leader who holds the group together. Unlike more traditional groups, which use similar motivational methods, the cults demand absolute loyalty, financial sacrifice, and complete rejection of former values. The 1978 mass suicide of 900 followers of Jim Jones at the People's temple in Guyana underscored the destructive consequences of a charismatic leader gone mad. While the Jonestown tragedy is an extreme case, thousands of other impressionable, well-meaning people have had their lives and finances stripped by cults.

Who Is Most Susceptible?

Herbert Simons has drawn a profile of the person most vulnerable to persuasion.[3] The easy mark tends to be younger rather than older, has average or below average intelligence and education, maintains a rigid belief system, has a low self-image, is bothered by complexity, and avoids problems. When the recruit first hears the message of the cult, he's delighted that the answers are so clear. He really needs to make only the one decision to follow the ideology of the group. His life seems clearly marked-out. The prospect of no more confusion and hassle is most reassuring. Tufts University psychiatrist Stanley Kath says, "Converts have to believe only what they are told. They don't have to think, and this relieves tremendous tensions."[4] Independent, critical thought is quickly labeled the tool of the devil and members are conditioned to follow the tenets and morality of the group.

Typical recruits are young people who are becoming more disenchanted with a way of life that seems phony and useless. Friends are seen as preoccupied with earning a college degree only to satisfy their insatiable lust for material possessions. Classes, endless parties and pursuit of the dollar have left a feeling of emptiness and near despair. Traditional religion offers little more than barren ritual and reinforcement of the same materialistic values. Recruits are highly vulnerable to appeals that promise a new and more noble way of life. Talk of helping the downtrodden and improving the human condition are part of the lure. Jim Jones didn't attract followers by talking about mass suicide or long hours of hard labor but by stressing service to the poor and the elimination of social injustice. This is very heady stuff for impressionable young people who are trying to shape their value system and who want to contribute to a better world.

While not all the members are under thirty, many fit that age category. Cult recruiters are particularly skilled in spotting a potential member. They often roam college campuses looking for the type of students most likely to accept the initial invitation to a special dinner. Their quarry are the lonely and depressed who find life confusing and difficult. Cult recruiters are especially adept at audience analysis. They often make their pitch at exam time because they know that a few students are depressed, burned out and looking for something more than books, teachers and fellow students, who seem materialistic and shallow. Cult recruits bask in the warmth they receive from new-found friends, and they like the certitude of the doctrine they hear. Recruits go through the process known in cult circles as "love bombing" in which they are showered with compliments and made to feel special.

Chris

Like Liz, Chris was vulnerable to cult tactics. He had just graduated from Yale but wasn't sure what he wanted to do. Disenchanted with his life in the east, he took a bus to California and found himself on the Berkeley campus. Within half an hour, a stocky young man with a big smile approached him and introduced himself as Jacob. Jacob invited Chris to a special dinner where he would meet other young people who were loving and idealistic.[5] Chris accepted and was pleasantly surprised by the warmth of the people he found there. His hosts showered him with compliments and made him feel more welcome here than he had felt anywhere in months. Some held his hands and others swathed him in a warm hug. Soon the entire group started singing songs and clapping in unison, their faces projecting what Chris later remembered as an orchestrated performance.

Near the end of the evening's fun and togetherness, three young men approached Chris and asked him if he would like to join this same group for a weekend in the country. He was told there would be fresh air, singing and volleyball. Still riding the crest of this happy first encounter, Chris accepted and found the retreat a pleasant extension of the dinner he had enjoyed so much. The group quickly involved him in games, singing sessions and abstract religious discussions. Retreat organizers didn't allow much time for sleep but he was having such a good time he didn't realize he was becoming tired and had stopped questioning some of the strange ideas he heard.

Soon a monitor was following him everywhere, even to the bathroom. On Monday morning, his recruiters asked him to stay for a full week and he said yes. By now, he had joined the ranks of the idealistic young people who get swallowed up by cults every year. Chris was recruited by the Moonies—the group which, some maintain, uses the most sophisticated persuasive techniques to recruit and keep members.

Liz and Chris both fit the profile of the typical cult recruit. They were young, idealistic and looking for answers they couldn't find from their friends, family or church. Each was groping for a sense of identity in a world that seemed meaningless. Thus, they became ripe for plucking by cult persuaders.

Characteristics of cults

Very few cults would use that word to describe themselves. Living in a country which allows free expression of thought and religion, cults simply maintain that they are enjoying their constitutional right and are really trying to help their members lead a better life. While they admit to using highly sophisticated methods of persuasion, they quickly retort they are no different from any other religion, especially during the crucial phase of training converts. In one sense, their claim is right. Stephen Hersh, the Assistant Director of the National Institute of Mental Health, maintains that the brainwashing tactics often linked to cults is, in most cases, just high pressure salesmanship. But there is a discernible pattern of persuasion which sets the cults apart. While the Marines and Benedictine Monks may utilize persuasive methods to win newcomers to their ideology, the level and kind of pressure is different.

Phase one of indoctrination includes an invitation to dinner or some pleasant social function in which the recruit is showered with compliments. If they fall for the opening gambit, members go through a two or three-day retreat without knowing exactly what they're getting into. Unlike military organizations or traditional religious orders, cults typically don't reveal who they are up-front. One ex-Moonie recalled: "If we had told them that we believed Moon was the Messiah or that we stayed up all night praying in the snow, they'd never join."[6] Only after the recruit has been led through the love-bombing and retreat stages does she learn what the group believes. By this time, the recruit is usually hooked. During the first two steps, new members hear only those ideas which sound noble and appealing. Who can argue with loving one's neighbor, trying to build a better world or fighting rampant materialism?

Unlike mainline churches, most cults seek to isolate their members from outside counter-ideas. The Children of God and Hare Krishna provide novices with new names in an effort to stamp out the past and identify completely with the new group. In a world dominated by materialism and greed, leaders present their band of followers as the one and only true source of salvation. Instructors warn members that family and friends will try to woo them back to their old decadent lifestyle.

Therefore, followers are trained in counter-persuasion tactics. Out-groups are called anything from "sugar-coated Christians" to "satanic." The cult has the "Truth" and the ticket to salvation. Anything else is riddled with error and should be scrupulously avoided.

The typical human is bombarded daily by about 1500 different messages which range from ads to buy cereals to appeals for money. Because the messages are so many and varied, it's easy to resist them. But when someone is subjected to the same basic message from the time he gets up to the moment he goes to bed, week after week, much of it sticks. Attention determines action, and what we attend to persuades us. If we're getting ideas only from one source, it doesn't take long to convert and stay in the fold.

Brainwashing

Most cults utilize techniques which border on brainwashing. The term "brainwashing" sounds mysterious and foreboding, with visions of wires strapped to the victim's head in an effort to drastically alter his mind. But brainwashing is an intense form of persuasion directed toward individuals who have been captured. The term was coined in 1951 by Robert Lifton who did studies on young American prisoners who were "brainwashed" by the Chinese Communists during the Korean war. Contrary to what many believe, brainwashing usually does not involve physical torture. Captors exert strong psychological pressure as they attempt to attack the prisoner's sense of self.[7]

Brainwashing includes three elements: dread, disability and dependence. Those captured are immediately placed in a state of anxiety and confusion. Captors often will fluctuate between a process of hard confrontation and a gentle easing up just when the prisoner expects to receive more intense questioning or further pressure. During the first stages of brainwashing, prisoners don't know what to expect. They fear for their lives and their captors do everything they can to enforce this notion. A prisoner might be hauled out of his cell at 2 o'clock in the morning, be brought to a questioning room and grilled for four or five hours. The ominous threat of torture and impending death hangs in the air, although neither is usually carried out. Victims are often deprived of sleep and nutritionally balanced food to dull their senses and reduce their power to think clearly.

Captors impose a strong dose of guilt on their victims and usually encourage confession for past faults and sins. Confessions provide release and also bond the prisoners more closely to their captors. Once the subject is "broken," he often feels an allegiance to the group that has put him through the excruciating experience.

Patty Hearst

Patrica Hearst is a good example of someone who was a victim of brainwashing. When she was 19, members of the Symbionese Liberation Army captured and imprisoned her in the dark closet of an old house. For two months she didn't know where she was and her captors constantly threatened her life. They also bombarded her with a series of messages which included a denunciation of the American capitalistic system. They constantly repeated that her wealthy parents symbolized most of the problems in the country. Like most victims of brainwashing, Patty Hearst resisted at first, but the relentless, hourly repetition of the same messages started to make in-roads in her mind. Little by little, she started to pay attention. Occasionally, a captor would offer a kindness which she gratefully accepted. Finally, after some weeks, she started believing what she heard and re-emerged as "Tania."

Americans were shocked to see Patty Hearst's picture in the paper and learn that she had joined her Symbionese captors in robbing a bank. Such a drastic conversion should not be surprising. Patty Hearst fits the profile of the easily persuadable victim who falls prey to a group which uses the intense, coercive tactics characteristic of cults. She was young, impressionable and was subjected to at least six weeks of brainwashing tactics.

Her attorney, F. Lee Bailey, used brainwashing as a defense in her trial for bank robbery. And even though she was convicted of robbing the bank, she was clearly a victim of brainwashing.[8]

It would be unfair to argue that all cults use the same kind of brainwashing tactics on their recruits as captors do on those prisoners they attempt to brainwash. The Chinese communists of the 50s and the Symbionese Liberation Army members are obviously different from the Moonies and Hare Krishna. But some of the methods are at least similar, and in some cases, very close. Lifton maintains that the same type of thought reform typical of prisoners during the Korean war can be found in some former cult members.[9]

Cult motivators reinforce a feeling of dread in their audience. The idealistic student may be preoccupied with losing her soul. Or the disillusioned 30-year-old businessman may feel profound emptiness as he ponders a profession which leaves ashes in his soul. Knowing this, the presenter reinforces the absolute necessity of changing one's lifestyle and ideas to avoid damnation or gain fulfillment. Rather than telling the recruit not to worry about salvation, the recruiter constantly tells members they're in imminent danger of losing their souls, unless they commit to the group. Instructors emphasize that all other organizations are tools of the devil and that only this church provides the salvation and peace the recruit yearns for.

After putting recruits through a process of dread and confusion, instructors work on disabling them psychologically. Mental defenses are broken down and the victim is now open to any new messages. Indoctrinators tell recruits repeatedly that the ideas they've learned are all wrong and that they must change their thinking to find salvation. Independent thought is considered a device of Satan. With the conviction and intensity of a drill sergeant, the mentor works to "wash out" the old ideas and replace them with the new. And such motivators hammer home the same theme: without us, there is no salvation.

Rhetorical theorist Kenneth Burke points out a discernible pattern which helps explain how cults persuade differently from mainline churches. According to Burke, a particular group of people are dis-enchanted and suffering either from a distinctive or vague sense of guilt. Perceiving this, the leader identifies the source of guilt and then im-mediately offers a scapegoat to expiate sins or ease a sense of failure. The scapegoat provides a legitimate outlet for aggression and pent-up frustra-tion. Burke illustrates his theory by describing Hitler's success in re-chan-neling the frustrations of many Germans in the early 30s. Many in that country still felt humiliated by Germany's defeat in World War I and were devastated by the poverty which resulted. Hitler offered a scapegoat in the Jews. Individuals and nations find it hard to accept responsibility, so they transfer the guilt to an out-group. A charismatic leader can effectively focus on "the enemy" and lay the blame on them.[10]

Most cult leaders name an outside enemy who is presumably ready to destroy the group unless members stay constantly alert. The "enemy" can be Jews, Communists, the government, parents who don't understand, or rival churches. By transferring the guilt of the members to the scapegoat, the members of the cult are able to gain catharsis for their sins. This purges them and allows them to regain some inner peace.

When Is a "Cult" Not a Cult?

A number of churches have been labeled cults. The Mormons, Jehovah's Witnesses, and Seventh Day Adventists have all been tagged with this unflattering title. But if a cult is defined more by its behavior and persuasive methods than its ideology, such a term seems inaccurate and unfair when applied to these churches. Orthodox Christians may disagree with the tenets of groups that don't share their theology, but *method,* not theology is the key difference. The Mormons and Jehovah's Witnesses, in particular, use intensive and often very effective motivational messages to gain converts and to keep the faithful, but they don't try to hide who they are. Neither do they isolate members from outside messages, try to smother any dissent or establish a scapegoat who becomes an outlet for aggression.

Protection from Cults

Your exuberant 17-year-old sister comes home and announces she has just attended a "fantastic dinner" put on by some people who "really care." Further, she has been invited to attend a three-day retreat the following week so she can learn wonderful ways to help change her life for the better. You learn that the group is a religious cult which specializes in recruiting impressionable young people. How would you convince her either not to attend the retreat or at least to counteract the influence of the group?

In a democratic society like the United States, the First Amendment guarantees freedom of speech. This, in turn, allows cult recruiters constant opportunities to gain new converts and to keep the old ones in line. While there has been some movement toward trying to establish legal protection for those who have been clearly hurt by coercive persuasion, the best safeguards are an awareness of tactics used by the cults and counter-persuasion methods.

Knowledge of what the cult stands for and the tactics they use is one of the best protections from getting hooked. Rather than trying to high-pressure a brother, sister, son or daughter into drawing back from a cult, the better approach would be to find the right time and place for a talk. Most people resent being told, "You're going to ruin yourself if you join that cult because they're a bunch of crazies! They chant, shave their heads and con people in airports." A quiet talk and a series of questions about the group is usually more productive. Who are they? What do they stand for? Who is their leader? Do they allow any criticism of their organization or their ideas? Do they encourage you to compare them to other religions and then make up your own mind?

There's an adage in sales: "If *you* say it, it might be true. If the person you're trying to persuade says it, it's absolutely true." Using a low-key questioning method works in other forms of motivation and it can be applied to counteracting the persuasive power of cults as well. If the potential recruit is willing to ask the cult the questions above and will not flinch at the answers, then the next step is to explain how cults persuade differently from most other organizations.

It's important to rechannel the potential member's idealism into something more constructive than what the cult offers. People are often vulnerable to the tactics of a cult because they're disillusioned over a life they consider empty and meaningless. A vacuum exists and no one is filling it. If all one does is tear down the cult and offers nothing in its place, the potential recruit is still open to the next movement to come along that promises a better way of life.

Finally, the vulnerable need a strong dose of love and concern from family and friends. The major magnet that draws members to the bizarre group is not the funky rituals, but the hope of love. The cults fill two voids: lack of love and lack of certainty about life's meaning. Any package which promises both is hard to resist. So counter-persuasion should contain the twin elements of love and meaning. If love conquers all, it's a powerful force in contending with cults.

Summary of Key Points

1. Cults are different from mainline churches, not because of their ideas or theology, but because of their behavior and persuasive methods.

2. Cult recruiters are particularly adept at targeting the most likely candidates for their organization. Such people usually include idealistic students, those with a low self-image, those whose lives have become complicated and who are looking for simple answers to complex questions, and people who are strongly disenchanted with their present situations.

3. Persuasive methods the cults typically use are:

a. Appeal to noble motives like helping the poor, changing society for the better, aiding one's fellow human, and finding a better and higher spiritual life.

b. Cults rarely reveal up-front who they are. The usual pitch includes statements like, "We're a group of people who really love each other and would like to change what we see as terrible injustices"—or, "We want to practice the gospel the way God really intends without watering it down." Only later do cult leaders inform followers who they are.

c. Indoctrinators try to strip away most past values derived from family or society and brand such values as evil, materialistic and tools of Satan. Constant repetition of this theme is crucial to keep recruits from wavering.

d. Members are isolated from outside messages until they have gone through intense persuasion techniques designed to secure their allegiance to the group.

e. Guilt and fear, especially of losing one's soul, are primary motivational tools for recruiting and keeping members. Instructions constantly reinforce the message that only the cult can provide salvation.

f. Instructors warn followers that family members will try to get them back. Then, the recruits are taught counter-persuasion methods designed to shut off all outside messages.

g. Cult leaders ask for total dedication to the group's ideology. This takes the form not only of mental and emotional commitment but often includes handing over any material possessions or financial assets. Such a request is usually presented as a "sign" that the member is serious about involvement.

h. Cults almost always battle an outside "enemy" which is out to destroy them. Such an enemy becomes a scapegoat to help absorb much of the blame for the evils so odious to the cult.

4. What to do:

a. Without badgering, ask the recruit questions. Let him explore the consequences of involvement with the group.

b. Empathize with the frustration and confusion usually present for someone vulnerable to cult tactics.

c. Give strong support and love.

8

The Persuasive Power of Film and Television: What To Do About It

The viewers sit in the darkened space transfixed by the images on the wall. When two of them cheer, the rest follow. Is this an enactment of Plato's "Cave" in *The Republic*? No, it's a Monday night at the movies crowd watching *Beverly Hills Cop II*. Despite the complete implausibility of plot and intensity of the violence, almost everyone cheers when the villains get splattered by Eddie Murphy and his two buddies from the Beverly Hills Police Force.

Sure, Eddie Murphy is a fine comedic actor, the action is fast-paced and the visual effects are entertaining. But the film is saturated with profanity, laced with constant violence and spiced with suggestive scenes which have little to do with the plot. In a fierce battle with television, the film industry offers ever more violence, sex and profanity to attract an audience.

So what's the harm, especially if there's an "R" rating to keep the kids out and adults can recognize the difference between fantasy and reality? According to psychologists Gordon Globus and Roy Shulman, the darkened environment of a theater lowers an audience's defenses and makes them more open to influence than usual.[1] During the day, the average person takes in thousands of fast-moving messages. But the movie-goer focuses for two hours on one engrossing story. Rarely will anyone have his attention riveted on one theme for as long. Movies are a unique and powerful form of persuasion because conflicting messages are banished for two hours.

The Power of the Electronic Media

Marshall McLuhan was an English professor who got tired of writing articles few people read. So he started to spin out provocative books about the power of the electronic media.[2] His "three ages of the media" and famous line that the "medium is the message" became familiar phrases in the 60s. McLuhan's theories also underscored the impact of the media as a persuasive power.

According to McLuhan, humans didn't need special methods of communicating at the dawn of history because they saw each other face to face. If you lived in a tribal village, you could discuss meals, hunting and mating directly. But then, tribesmen started their own villages and this produced a demand for other ways to communicate. Instead of direct conversation, smoke signals informed another village that the party was on for Saturday night or that they were going to be attacked the next day. Clothing became an extension of the skin, the wheel an extension of the foot, and smoke signals an extension of the voice.

In 1436, the German Johannes Gutenberg invented movable type and printed copies of the Bible. This event revolutionized the way people could communicate. In the old system, monks had to labor long and hard over manuscripts to get one copy. But the invention of printing put pamphlets and books in the hands of thousands. Jean Rousseau's two works, *Discourse on the Inequalities of Men* and *Social Contract,* helped fan the flames of the French revolution in the latter part of the 18th century. Thomas Paine's pamphlet, "Common Sense," became a spark for the American Revolution.

The Gutenberg era paled by comparison to the age of the electronic media. Samuel Morse invented the telegraph, and the telephone, radio, and film followed. Then came the most powerful medium of all—television. TV was woven into the fabric of anyone's life who could afford a set.

Many households kept it glowing from early morning until late into the night. Television created a global village where viewers could know instantaneously what's going on in the world. TV also became a dominant force in most households. In the old days, tribesmen sat around mesmerized by the flames of the fire in the center of the village. Today, family members sit and gaze at television for hours. Just try to walk into the middle of "Days of Our Lives" or "General Hospital" and interrupt the devotees. Normally civil people respond with "Hush, Justin's finally going to get what he deserves," or "Puleeze, do we have to talk right now?! I'll take care of your broken arm later!"

Television changed the way we saw the universe. During World War II, most Americans learned about battles through patriotic newsreels, John Wayne movies and newspapers supporting the American side. Everyone believed the issues were clear-cut and that the cause was just. Very few citizens protested during the Second World War. Messages were one-dimensional—we're right and they're wrong. Who could sit in a darkened theater and watch John Wayne storm the hill at Iwo Jima and not be spurred on to win the war? Anti-war films were virtually non-existent.

But during the Vietnam conflict, all the patriotic coverage changed to a cold, realistic look at war and millions didn't like what they saw. Viewers watched U. S. Marines walk into a village of straw-thatched huts and burn it to the ground. They listened to influential commentators who doubted we were in a war we could win. A steady stream of news programs reconfirmed the message that America was bogged down in a conflict it didn't want but didn't know how to finish.

Presidents Nixon and Johnson couldn't persuade the American public to accept their reassurances that the U. S. was making progress in Vietnam because air time was stacked against them 10 to 1. Nixon went on TV to explain his rationale for a military excursion into Cambodia, and immediately afterward three articulate newscasters dissected his speech and criticized his policy. Walter Cronkite, one of the most influential motivators of the 60s, went to Vietnam and returned with the message that despite what the government was saying, there was no "light at the end of the tunnel" and "America was not winning the war." Who would most citizens believe—a President they didn't trust or a highly respected and well-liked commentator? Media personalities replaced politicians as the major wielders of influence.

Why is the Electronic Media so Powerful?

For anyone who watched the event on TV, the pictures are still burned in the mind. On May 4, 1970, student protestors at Kent State confronted a group of youthful National Guardsmen and shots filled the air. Four of the protestors fell to the ground, victims of bullets from the reluctant guns. Few who saw the scene will forget the picture of the grieving, enraged girl bending over her fallen companion and crying to the skies for justice.

If the Kent State killings had been reported only in the papers, the furor would not have been so dramatic and far-reaching. But millions participated by watching the shootings first-hand. Then they turned to their TV sets for stories about the mass rebellion that followed. College classes around the country shut down as students protested the deaths of their fallen brothers and sisters. More than any other single event, the Kent State killings mobilized draft age Americans against the war.

Most people can pinpoint what they were doing the moment radio and television announced that John Kennedy had been shot. I was teaching a high school English class and heard the principal's voice over the loudspeaker tell us that the President had been felled by an unknown assassin who fired from a Texas book depository. The death of Kennedy galvanized everyone and television put us all in Parkland hospital during Kennedy's last moments. We watched that weekend as an incredible drama played itself out on the screen. Lee Harvey Oswald was captured and then gunned down in the basement of the Dallas jail by a strip joint owner named Jack Ruby. The cameras followed the fatal confrontation of Oswald meeting Ruby and picked up the muffled shots as Oswald twisted in the arms of a Texas lawman.

Television highlighted the transfer of Kennedy's body back to Washington, D.C. Viewers were there on the plane for the swearing-in of the new president Lyndon Johnson as Kennedy's widow Jackie looked on. The same television cameras let us attend the funeral and the impact was little different from the death-watch for a family member. The same cameras lingered over the poignant small figure of John Kennedy, Jr., saluting his father's casket as it passed by in solemn procession.

TV brings us in close to the action and often gives us a better view than spectators at the scene. Television becomes a friend in the middle of the night when we can't sleep. The dial-flipper can watch a snippet of a Cary Grant movie, a pitch for an amazing face cream that will "change your face and your life," a call to turn from sin and send money issued by a silver-haired, well coifed evangelist, and catch the last ten seconds of a college basketball game—all in one minute. At 2 a.m., TV cuts through the darkness and brings human faces into the room.

Media Power and Viewing Time

Between grades one and twelve, the average American student will spend over ten thousand hours watching television and films and five thousand hours in class. Most people are astounded to learn that Americans average 6.3 hours per day watching television and that the typical family has the set on ten hours over a 24-hour period. Children and teenagers aren't the only ones who contribute to the national average. Many adults use this familiar friend to escape stress, to be entertained and to learn.

TV and movies are persuasive media but each has a different impact. In sheer time, television wins by a wide margin. Except for professional film watchers like Siskel and Ebert, most people don't spend hours watching movies. But TV can dominate a day. During the average six hours, a viewer can see two soaps, four game shows, the news and three evening sitcoms. On weekends, throw in two football games, a 1950s movie, "60 Minutes," and a local talk show. If viewers' ideas, attitudes and morals are controlled by what they attend to, TV has to be one of the most persuasive forces in our society.

Two-Edged Swords

Television and film are two-edged swords. Each can help or hurt anyone who spends time watching. On the plus side, television and movies have helped prevent nuclear war because the media has brought home the horror of war in graphic detail. In pre-electronic media days, you couldn't see your enemy and the only messages people received about the war were the ones their leaders wanted them to see and hear. During the Third Reich, Germans focused on Hitler's message of hate and glory because propaganda minister Goebbels had complete control of the media. Massive outdoor rallies, radio broadcasts, newspapers and pamphlets reinforced only the one Nazi message. But in the television era, especially in a free society, citizens get to watch, listen and vicariously participate in all aspects of war. Before TV, most leaders could get their followers to go to war primarily because they were able to focus only on the positive aspects of battle. But television news coverage highlights the horrors of war and does very little to promote the glory.

Movies like *The Day After* and *Testament* leave the viewer not only drained but determined to do whatever is needed to avoid a nuclear holocaust. Images of the first brain-numbing blast, radiation sickness and the long, dark winter are grafted in the viewer's mind. After watching the horror on TV, only a madman could conclude that a nuclear war is a glorious event.

Ironically, while television and films helped fan the flames of the sexual revolution, both media have also helped in highlighting one of the effects of sexual activity—the AIDS epidemic. Physician Marshall Goldberg has emphasized, "TV has done more to contain AIDS than any other single factor."[3] In a continuous mosaic of educational programs, films and documentaries, television has reinforced the dangers of casual sex.

Three Key Messages

Despite its power for good, at least three messages permeate the media: (1) violence is a way to solve problems (2) sex is natural and should be enjoyed outside of marriage, and (3) material possessions are the key to happiness. Such messages are not presented as clearly as a commercial, but one has only to watch TV over two days to absorb the triple themes.

Violence

If your name is Rambo, and someone slaps you on the right cheek, go back two years later with the most lethal weapons you can find and destroy him, his family and his village. If you're a muscle-bound commando with an Austrian accent and someone kidnaps your only daughter, make sure you crush, strangle and shoot everyone connected to the evil deed. If you're *Dirty Harry,* never mind the law—even if you're a cop yourself. Bash any unsavory character who stands in your way. Except in movies like *Ghandi,* there is little talk of turning the other cheek or using non-violence as a deliberate strategy for solving human problems. Christ has said, "Don't resist violence! If you are slapped on one cheek, turn the other, too." "Love your enemies. Pray for those who persecute you." This key Christian theme is rarely heard or seen in the media.

Viewers can watch *Robocop* on one night and *Beverly Hills Cop II* the next and at least 50 problems have been stamped out by guns, knives, and explosives. Most people realize that movies and television programs are fantasies, but some find it hard to make the distinction. These highly impressionable viewers find the line between fantasy and reality blurred and conclude that violence is a sure way to solve conflict with people who cross you. Most viewers can walk out of a movie or away from a TV set and not be moved to action by the intense violence they've just seen. But, take an impressionable, slightly off-center person who is frustrated with life, and violence offers a solution for his bottled-up aggression.

Children and teenagers, in particular, are vulnerable to films and TV programs depicting violence. As many weave their way through the jagged rocks of adolescence in their search for identity, they're open to anything that will provide an outlet for their frustration. The *American Journal of Pediatrics* states that by the time a teenager leaves high school, he will have seen 18,000 murders on television. Spokane doctor Jim States, an expert on adolescent behavior, maintains, "We as adults encourage our kids to be violent."[4]

The evidence is overwhelming that TV and movie violence spawns violent behavior in those who are vulnerable to it. In a study comparing the effects of television watching to aggression, L. Rowell Huesmann, Lirsti Lagerspertz and Leonard Eron found that certain children respond forcefully to the violence they see on the screen.[5] The researchers concluded that the combination of predisposition plus constant viewing leads to violent behavior in some children. Young people who watch violent programs often, who identify closely with aggressive heroes and who themselves are unpopular, tend to solve their own problems in violent ways.

Most children can watch the violent cartoon or movie and won't go out and commit a crime. But fuse a low self-image with a proclivity toward aggression, problems in school, plus unpopularity with peers, and television can become the match that lights the bonfire of aggression.

Sex

If violence dominates TV, so does sex. In a typical hour, the viewer can see 27 examples of sexual behavior which include nine kisses, five embraces, ten sexual innuendos and at least one reference to intercourse.[6] Sex is an obvious fact of life, but the message is constantly transmitted that sex should be enjoyed anytime the opportunity presents itself.

"LA Law" is one of the better programs on television but almost all the attorneys have affairs with little or no discussion about morals. Hey, if it feels right, do it—as long as you use condoms. Most daytime soaps weave the same message into their plots. Try to find a heated conversation about the morality of sex outside of marriage. All you need to make it right is attraction and a spare room or a cabin by the lake. Conversations on "Days of Our Lives," "General Hospital," and "As the World Turns" now include the need to protect against AIDS, but rarely if ever do the characters discuss values relating to monogamy, marital commitment, or the Ten Commandments.

The sexual revolution has come and gone and has left in its wake some disillusioned devotees who have concluded that indiscriminate sex can kill. But the fear of AIDS hasn't really made most viewers re-evaluate their sexual morals. The epidemic has given practical-minded Americans a chance to find a way to have sex without getting the fatal infection. Television programs and films have been a boon to the condom industry as lovers try to figure out how to deal with but not stop extra-marital sex.

Grabbing the Good Life

He's a single, 36-year-old financial adviser who earns $50,000 a year. He should have it made, but he doesn't. He owes $50,000—$10,000 on his assorted charge cards, $30,000 in student loans and $10,000 to his father. [7] This professional with a doctoral degree represents many Americans who spend more than they make and plunge deeper into debt each year. With millions of consumers forced to use half of their take-home salary to pay off debts, something is wrong. Harvard psychiatrist Ned Hallowell states that just about everyone is overspending.[8] Is television one cause of runaway credit spending? It would be unfair to dump all the blame on TV, but the media plays a part.

Many television programs and films send an unmistakable message: if you want to be happy, collect as many Jaguars, beach-front houses, diamonds, vacation trips and other luxuries as you can. Such is the ticket to bliss. The more you get, the happier you'll be. Rarely do programs convey the theme that happiness is found in loving others and sharing material wealth with the needy. The message is hammered home in numerous ways: "you only go around once," "grab for the gusto," "living well is the best revenge."

Christ told His followers not to store treasures on earth where they can erode or be stolen. They should be stored in heaven where they will never lose their value and are safe from thieves. If our profits are in heaven, our heart will be there too. He went on to emphasize how difficult it is to serve God and money.[9] Such a message rarely comes across on commercial television.

Visual Orientation

Steve comes home after a hard day. He's bushed and stressed out. So he turns on the TV five minutes after pouring himself a beer. He has no idea what he'll see and goes through an evening ritual of flipping seven channels in the course of one minute. He finds something that has mild appeal and plops himself in front of the TV for the next four hours. Finally, it's time to go to bed and get ready for another rough day. Mindless TV watching has become a way of life for many people. Besides offering a reassuring voice and soothing color, television provides an escape. But continuous television watching without any purpose creates a habit that is hard to break. Steve is becoming a "visual."

Neurolinguists claim that humans are oriented in one of three ways: visually, auditorially and kinesthetically.[10] Some people learn best by seeing, others by hearing and others by touching. Television has swung the national average toward the side of the visual. If the average student spends twice as much time in front of the tube as he does in his grade or high school classroom, he forms habits of mind which are hard to break. Ask him to read and he looks at you as if you had suggested he clean the oven with a toothbrush.

In *The Closing of the American Mind*, Allan Bloom states: " . . . whatever the cause, our students have lost the practice and taste for reading. They have not learned how to read, nor do they have the expectation of delight or improvement from reading."[11] Many students have dined on a steady diet of television and therefore are not used to the more satisfying taste of the printed word. Reading in school is considered a bore and is often endured only because of an impending exam. A few have discovered the deep joy that comes from immersion in a good book, but the majority prefer TV.

Habits of mind are formed early and if a child gets into the habit of reading, she will most likely continue to read the rest of her life. If a three-year-old gets stationed in front of the tube and sits for hours watching everything from "Sesame Street" to "Wheel of Fortune," she finds it hard to love reading later. Television too often becomes a convenient babysitter for hassled parents who are trying to juggle a career and family life.

What To Do

Any habit is hard to change, but TV viewing is one of the hardest. The crusading parent who storms into the family room and annnounces that TV will be drastically cut back gets hooted out of the house. But some approaches work:

1. Spend time reading with your children. Let them read to you and return the favor. This not only provides a sense of bonding, but also gets them into a habit that will be one of the most important in their lives. TV watching will not go away and it would be naive to assume that it will. But early exposure to books will reap rich benefits later in academic success and enjoyment from the printed word.

2. Discuss your own moral views about violence and sex when episodes appear on TV. Brace yourself for comments like "dweeb," "old fashioned" and "out of it," but realize that such conversations at least provide a moral perspective different from the stories spun on the tube.

3. Pick programs in advance. While some families have gone cold-turkey on television, such a move is unrealistic for most. But you can be selective in your own television viewing. One time-saver is to scan the TV guide or newspaper listing of television programs for the week and decide how many hours you want to put in. Then, pick the programs you consider not only entertaining but uplifting. It's easy to get in the habit of turning on

the set and sponging up whatever appears. Encourage children to choose quality programs.

Rank's Model

Hugh Rank[12] has devised a model which helps people arm themselves against persuasive messages they don't want. Effective persuaders get an audience to focus on the good points of a product, candidate or idea and ignore the bad ones. Therefore, Rank suggests that when a message emphasizes positive features, the person wanting to resist should immediately think of all the bad points. Let's say you're watching TV and suddenly you're confronted by the most beautiful wool-cashmere coat you've ever seen. Better yet, this coat, normally $550, is on sale for $350 in *the* quality story. Immediately your mind starts conjuring up the tremendous savings and the pleasure you will have in wearing the coat you really want. But you stop and remember a resolve not to buy anything else this month. You already have an attractive, serviceable coat and you're getting close to maxing out your Visa card. But the tug of the coat is almost too much. The combination of sale and quality merchandise is strong. So what do you do? If you really want to protect yourself and resist the pitch, focus immediately on all the disadvantages of buying the coat—a deeper plunge into credit, a nagging feeling of remorse that's sure to follow and disappointment with yourself for giving in again. Also, concentrate on your resolve not to overspend. Then enjoy the feeling of victory.

Summary of Key Points

1. Television and movies wield great persuasive power. The average person is motivated by what he attends to and he attends to many hours of TV and movie watching each week.

2. Television and movies can help or hurt. On the plus side, they have helped create a global village by bringing viewers directly to the action of

world events. Television has been instrumental in helping prevent nuclear war and the spread of AIDS.

3. But television and movies often provide relentless messages which include:

a. Violence is an effective way to solve human conflicts.

b. Sex outside of marriage is natural and should be enjoyed whenever possible, as long as no one gets hurt or catches a disease.

c. Material possessions are the keys to happiness.

4. TV has made many people more visually oriented. This makes it hard for them to enjoy reading.

5. If parents want to help their children use the media wisely, they can:

a. Get children into early habits of reading for pleasure so TV doesn't have the grip it does with many.

b. Discuss with family members moral issues that relate to violence, sex and material possessions.

c. Pick programs in advance to avoid the "random viewing" syndrome which wastes so much time.

6. Apply Rank's model to any undesired persuasive message. When a program reinforces an unacceptable message, downplay it. When a program downplays a message you believe in, focus on the benefits and your point of view.

9

The Persuasive Politician

A few years ago, Robert Redford starred in a movie called *The Candidate*. The story began with a group of professional campaign strategists who were disgruntled because their bland politician had lost another election. In frustration, they chose a man who had the charm, good looks, and the right image which Redford embodies. The movie went on to chronicle the candidate's rise from obscurity to national prominence through a slick and carefully orchestrated media plan. In the ironic ending, after winning the election, Redford turned to his campaign manager and asked, "What do I do now?"

The film was based on real-life politicians who were chosen by their party not because they were the best qualified, but because they projected the right image. If television helps sell cosmetics, soap and light beer, it's a boon for candidates who can be packaged and sold to voters.

The Candidate underscores a basic dilemma in American politics. On the one hand, effective politicians have to be skilled motivators, not only to get elected, but to argue for their constituents back home. Their primary tool is persuasion and if they don't know how to convince, they won't do their job well. On the other hand, millions vote for politicians merely because they're likable and not because they're the brightest and the best. While many voters carefully study the issues and the candidates, millions of others vote simply because they *like* a candidate. They respond positively to the way she looks or sounds, his smile or her engaging way of making an audience laugh. Rarely do the majority of voters carefully sift through campaign pamphlets to learn more about a candidate's background, stands on issues or ability to do the job better than the opposition. This is understandable because there are so many issues and candidates in most elections that it's hard to keep up. As a result, fluff and image become more decisive than substance and strong qualifications.

Do We Really Get the Best Qualified Public Officials?

Imagine a computer program that could identify the top 200 leaders in this country and then refine the list to the top 20. Imagine further that a group of experts (who themselves would be determined by computer analysis) would then pick the top two in the land for president and vice president. The other eighteen could take over cabinet jobs and serve in Congress.

While such an idea might repel most Americans, many would agree that only a small number of currently elected officials would make the top 200 list. Almost all incumbents were elected because they're capable persuaders who convinced citizens to vote for them. Many officials have other qualities—intelligence and experience—but persuasion got them where they are today.

Persuasion and Politics

As far back as ancient Athens, persuasion and politics have been compatible partners. Persuasion usually thrives in a democracy since any citizen is allowed to speak. In a dictatorship, only the dictator has the right of free speech so those people with a different view keep it to themselves.

In ancient Athens, a clever sophist named Gorgias seized an opportunity to do some moonlighting. Gorgias was the ambassador from Sicily who dazzled the Athenians with his rhetorical magic. Trained by Corax, the founder of the first known school of rhetoric, Gorgias established courses in the art of influencing. He quickly signed up prominent Greeks who recognized that their success as politicians or lawyers was in direct proportion to their ability to argue in court or in the Assembly of 500—the legislative body of Greek government. Athens in 450 B.C. was ripe for a teacher who would help candidates get elected to office and aid them in staying once they had won the election.

Athens was a "polis," or Greek city-state which meant it didn't have to answer to any higher governmental power. This democratic form of government held distinctive benefits for the citizens who comprised one-third of the population. (The other two-thirds were slaves.) If you wanted power in ancient Athens, you tried to get elected to office as a member of the Assembly of 500. Politicians had plenty of time to prepare campaigns and sharpen their persuasive skills: there were enough slaves around to do the mundane tasks. Athens became the Golden Age of Greece partially because citizens had so much time to make speeches, write poetry, and compose drama.

Plato denounced the use of rhetoric in Athens because he saw it primarily as a tool which allowed glib politicians to gain and hold power. In Plato's view, most rulers were bogged down in the cave of a passing material world and could care less about leading themselves or their followers to the more exalted life of the spirit.

Twentieth century America and 5th century B.C. Athens share some common traits. Both have utilized persuasion to campaign and govern. Both have offered citizens the chance to speak on important issues. Each can boast of statesmen who were dedicated public servants and who served their constituents well. But each also has featured politicians whose rise to power was more a product of their silver tongue rather than a bright mind or proven leadership qualities.

Like other forms of influencing, political persuasion can be a help or a hindrance. On the positive side, elected officials who can't motivate are virtually useless. Imagine a President who couldn't negotiate with the Soviets or members of the Senate who couldn't convince their colleagues. But there's a reverse side and unless voters are careful, they can get taken just as quickly as an unwary customer buying a used car with the odometer turned back.

The Positive Side of Persuasion and Politics

A political campaign without persuasion is like a baseball game without a bat, tennis without a racquet or hockey without a puck. In a democratic system, politicians have to woo voters in a campaign and persuasion is the means they use. In the 1980s, candidates have to start at least a year in advance trying to convince citizens to vote for them. During the process, they come under intense public scrutiny as they move from primary to primary, constantly trying to persuade voters that they're best qualified to do the job. With television, citizens watch closely how candidates fare under pressure. Do they wilt when they get a tough question? Can they stand up under the sheer physical pressure of days which begin at six in the morning and often go until after midnight? Can they field complex, tricky questions and make the answers appear clear and sensible? Can they communicate their ideas well—a prerequisite for representing their constituents? Can their wives or husbands take the heat of blistering questions from the press and not flinch? Can they stand the glare of inquiries about their personal life and come out unscathed? If they're not good persuaders, they won't get elected.

Since the power to persuade is a prerequisite for election, candidates have to prove they can influence a wide variety of people. During the courting process of a campaign, politicians have to cajole, inspire and captivate voters. If they can't influence on the road to victory, they won't be effective after they arrive.

Once in office, persuasion becomes one of the politician's primary tools for getting the job done. Leaders who don't have the skills won't last. Not only do elected officials have to convince voters but they have to persuade each other. One of the distinctive features of the Constitution is the balance of power between legislative, judicial and executive. The President has to convince Congress that his bills are in the public good. Congressmen have to persuade the president that their proposals are sound. And judges must support their opinions with solid evidence and reasoning. Persuasion is intricately woven into the fabric of government and produces great benefits for its citizens.

While most voters are far better educated than they were back in the eighteenth century, few have the persuasive skills of most politicians. Candidates gain office mainly because they're so good at convincing people.

Debates as a Test of Persuasive Leadership

Debate offers one forum for separating persuasive politicians from pretenders. In 1858, Abraham Lincoln challenged Stephan Douglas to a debate in the hotly contested Illinois senatorial race. Even though Douglas won re-election, the debates greatly helped Lincoln's march toward the White House. Lincoln's debating skills marked him as a persuasive leader. John Kennedy, Jimmy Carter and Ronald Reagan all gained from their televised debates. But why are the debates so persuasive and helpful in the election process? For starters, debates offer voters the chance to carefully watch politicians under extreme pressure. With a national audience looking on and studio lights glaring on their faces, candidates must not only present their own point of view but also defend themselves from attacks by opponents. A slip can be fatal. Gerald Ford's emphatic statement that an Eastern European country was not under the domination of the Soviets was the turning point in the 1976 campaign and became a key factor in Jimmy Carter's election.

Debates are not the only forum which can help or ruin a candidate. Politicians have to walk gingerly through the mine-field of challenges that face them daily. They have to use the English language very carefully. A word or phrase can do them in as quickly as the April sun melts a late spring snow. Barry Goldwater helped dismantle his own drive toward the presidency in 1964 when he proclaimed during his convention acceptance speech that "Extremism in the defense of liberty is no vice! . . . Moderation in the pursuit of justice is no virtue!"[1] Many interpreted the statement as a defense of the John Birch element in the Republican Party and a repudiation of party moderates. George Romney sounded his own political death knell when he returned from Vietnam and announced that he had been "brainwashed." George McGovern came to regret his statement that he was one thousand percent behind Thomas Eagleton, especially since he reversed his position within the next few weeks, following Eagleton's nomination as vice-presidential candidate. Jimmy Carter's race to the White House was temporarily stalled by his "ethnic purity" remark and his comment in a *Playboy* interview that he "lusted in his heart." If sticks and stones can break your bones, in a political campaign they can really hurt you.

Candidates who can withstand the pressure of debates, speeches, interviews, and twelve-hour days, demonstrate their leadership qualities. If they can convince voters, despite the constant glare of media scrutiny, they often deserve to be elected.

The Negative Side

But there's a down-side to politics and persuasion. The same tactics used to get consumers to buy products are applied to win votes. Professional campaign strategists know that most citizens vote because they *like* and *trust* a politician, and not because they've carefully studied the issues and made a voting decision based on what they've found. Cosmetics and the inconsequential become more important for many voters than issues.

Richard Gephardt's eyebrows and Paul Simon's earlobes often received more attention in the 1988 race than the trade deficit or supplying arms to the Contras. Rebecca Nappi notes that "Campaign 1988" was obsessed with body parts: Gephardt's bland eyebrows versus Massachusetts Governor Michael Dukakis' bushy ones. Forget military spending, arms control, or the trade imbalance. Did Gephardt dye his eyebrows or not?[2] TV and video producer Ed Coker concludes that voters often focus on physical attributes like eyebrows and earlobes to avoid the real issues in a campaign.

"People feel overwhelmed. They think 'I'll look at their pictures and decide who I like.'"[3]

Saying What Voters Want to Hear

Perennial tongue-in-cheek candidate Pat Paulsen gives a standard speech every time he enters a new city. If he's "campaigning" in Des Moines, Iowa, he compliments the crowd on their fine city and says he plans to retire in Des Moines. He describes people in Des Moines as so much more genuine than folks in Los Angeles where he lives. Then he moves on to Eugene, Oregon, and tells the Oregonians what a beautiful city they have and that he plans to make his home there just as soon as he retires. He emphasizes that Eugene is so much nicer, cleaner and fresher than Los Angeles with its smog and congested freeways. He repeats basically the same line in all the cities he visits. Finally, when reporters interview him after his triumphant return in Los Angeles, he tells the crowd there how happy he is to be home in Los Angeles—the greatest city in the world, a place he'll never leave because it has so much to offer and the people are so "real."

Paulsen is a caricature of politicians who will say whatever is needed to get votes. After they win the election, many officials seem to ignore what they promised so eloquently just a few weeks before.

Some wag invented a sure-fire way for detecting whether a politician is telling the truth. According to the test, if a politician stands looking directly at his audience with his left hand on his left hip—he's probably telling the truth. If he touches his nose with his right index finger—he's probably telling the truth. If he places both hands on his hips, he's most likely telling the truth. But if he opens his mouth . . .

The preceding may be unfair to many honest politicians, but voters have been fooled often enough to stop trusting candidates who promise more than they can deliver. Many are so disenchanted with the process that they have simply stopped voting.

Mud Slinging

Most campaigns over the years have begun with a promise from candidates that the races will be conducted on a high level. But such promises are short-lived. In the old days, politicians would save their mud slinging until the final two weeks before the election. Today, with the glare of the media and increased competition, the mud starts flying early. Robert Dole and George Bush started blasting each other in February of 1988. Even though the cadre of Democratic candidates softened their attacks on each other, mud slinging has remained a part of the American political ritual. Why?

It's often more effective to stimulate people *against* something or someone than to make them respond positively. Many voters find the diatribes and name-calling entertaining. The more intense the in-fighting and the smell of blood, the better the coverage. To hold the attention of an electorate saturated with political rhetoric, candidates are virtually forced to increase the intensity of their broadsides against each other. The closer the race, the more pointed the name-calling. Politicians far ahead in the polls can afford to be gracious to the faltering underdog. Those running a close race can't.

Two other aspects help distinguish politics from other ways of influencing. These two techniques are neither good nor bad but they help explain how motivation works in a campaign. The two techniques are the "two-stage" flow and the use of humor.

Two-Stage Flow

Word of mouth is still one of the best ways to motivate. If voters are doubtful about candidates and issues, they'll trust the viewpoint of someone they consider a leader. But where does the leader gather her information? Most often she gets it from television, radio, magazines and newspapers and then passes it on to others. She's a voracious reader who scoops up information from the *Wall Street Journal, Atlantic Monthly,*

Time, and *Newsweek.* She watches "Nightline" and "Meet the Press" on a regular basis. She listens to public radio on her way to work.

A busy professional is wavering about a candidate for the state legislature and feels overwhelmed by the blizzard of data on the issues. At a party, he gets into a conversation with the woman described above. She tells him she's going to vote for politician "A" and then goes on to discuss in detail port districts, dog control and revenue sharing. The professional is impressed with her command of the facts and her assurance about her voting decisions.

The woman is considered an opinion-leader primarily because she's knowledgeable about the campaign. And she absorbed such knowledge from the media. This phenomenon has been called the "two-stage" flow and it underscores the power of the media in contributing to what many consider the most effective kind of persuasion—word of mouth.[4] Followers typically receive most of their information directly from television and do very little reading. Leaders read much more but they also watch television and listen to the radio. They immerse themselves in news and commentary type programs. Rarely will they be caught curled up watching "Wheel of Fortune" or reruns of "SWAT." And often they're perceived as leaders because they seem to know much more about politics than their peers who get their data primarily from TV.

Most shrewd politicians know the power of leaders in swaying voters. Therefore, they court and cultivate opinion-leaders. Often, the chairperson of a campaign is chosen for proven and well-known leadership qualities rather than for the promise of hard work and long hours. When voters are undecided, they can always tune into how their leaders are voting and follow suit.

Humor

He was struggling in the debates with his opponent, but one line saved him. When Ronald Reagan said, "I will not let my opponent's youth and inexperience become an issue in this campaign" the audience howled. The president turned the tables on quipsters who highlighted his age as a liability. In recalling the four debates in 1984, viewers rarely remember the issues discussed, but recall well-timed retorts. Humor is a potent weapon for the politician who uses it well and a liability for one who can't. Recognizing the close link between humor and likability, many politicians work hard to polish their comedic skills. Some hire laugh writers to spice up their campaign speeches and fill their file with one-liners.

Why is humor such an effective persuasive device for politicians? We like people who make us laugh and we enjoy the feeling that comes from the well-told joke or the humorous story. Michael LeBoeuf points out that there are basically four emotions—glad, mad, sad and scared.[5] Successful motivators tap into the glad category: make people feel good and they're more open to your efforts to influence them.

Despite growing problems during his second term, Ronald Reagan remains a likable man. Much of this comes from his cultivated warmth, but he uses his actor's timing to tell the right story. This in turn softens his audience and makes them receptive to whatever else he wants to tell them.

Reagan told the following joke during a bill-signing ceremony at the Central Intelligence Agency: The story is that there was an agent overseas who happened to be in Ireland and there was an emergency and it was necessary to contact him immediately. So they called in another agent and they said, "Now, you'll go there. His name is Murphy and your recognition will be to say, 'Tis a fair day but it'll be lovelier this evening'."

So he went to Ireland—to a little town, where he went into the pub, elbowed himself up to the bar, ordered a drink and then asked the bartender, "How would I get in touch with Murphy?"

And the bartender says, "Well, if it's Murphy the farmer you want, it's two miles down the road and it's the farm on the left." He said, "If it's Murphy the bootmaker, he's on the second floor of the building across the street. And he says, "My name is Murphy."

So the agent picked up his drink and said, "Well, 'tis a fair day, but it'll be lovelier this evening."

"Oh," said the bartender, "it's Murphy the *spy* you want."[6]

Congressman Tom Foley is another politician who knows how to use humor to warm an audience and make his points. Foley has told the story about the politician who went into a somewhat conservative farming community and faced the question, "Congressman, what's your stand on *booze*?" Not knowing the political stance of his audience, the quick thinking politician replied, "If you're talking about demon rum which makes grown men squander their paycheck in the bars, I'm totally against it. But if you're referring to the wine produced by the grapes harvested from this area, I'm all for it. And that's my unequivocal stand on that subject."

People who make us laugh are attractive. Politicians who know how to use self-effacing humor are far more likable than their pompous and indifferent counterparts. The candidate who has made a voter laugh with a well-timed quip, will often get the nod over someone who has given a detailed explanation of the trade deficit. Laugh and the world laughs with you. Get people to smile and you often get their vote.

A Final Word on Politics and Persuasion

The right to vote is one of the key privileges of a democracy. It's also a right many voters take for granted. Some believe their vote doesn't really count. History is loaded with examples of crucial elections that turned on a single vote. In 1776, one vote determined that America would use the English language instead of German. In 1845, a single vote brought Texas into the Union. In 1923, one vote handed Adolph Hitler the leadership of the Nazi Party. In 1941, two weeks before Pearl Harbor, the Selective Service was salvaged by one vote.[7] Voters can apply the same yardsticks to politics as wise consumers do to buying products. A knowledge of the issues and a study of strategies should make a good system better. Ignorance and apathy will almost surely make it worse.

Summary of Key Points

1. Persuasion and politics have been closely linked for centuries. Persuasion thrives in a democratic society because politicians must convince citizens to vote for them.

2. On the plus side, campaigns provide excellent arenas for voters to observe politicians. If candidates can persevere in the pressure-cooker of a campaign, they demonstrate they have what it takes to provide strong representation for their constituents.

3. On the minus side, a candidate's power to persuade can often hide flaws and defects. Fluff and image become more decisive in the outcome of some elections than those qualities which make good leaders. Such qualities include clear thinking, problem-solving skills and decisiveness.

4. The "two-stage flow" is an important feature of political persuasion. The "two-stage flow" reaffirms that word-of-mouth persuasion is often the most effective and underscores the importance of opinion leaders and the media in a campaign.

5. Humor can greatly enhance the rapport between candidate and voters. Candidates who can adroitly use humor are perceived as more likable and as a consequence, are usually more persuasive.

6. Voters can apply the same standards to politicians as they do to salespeople and products. A careful study of candidates and issues provides the best protection from getting stuck with politicians who win votes on their personalities. Warmth and humor are fine, but experience, leadership and personal integrity offer the best chance for getting the strongest public officials.

10

Final Words and Guidelines

The audience was well educated and should have known better. But 55 psychologists, psychiatrists and social workers sat and listened to a speech delivered by "Dr. Myron Fox of the Albert Einstein University." Afterwards, hearers described the speaker as "excellent, extremely articulate, and warm." All reported they had learned something from the talk entitled "Mathematical game theory as applied to physical education." The speech was a mosaic of meaningless, contradictory statements coated with academic jargon. No one in the audience spotted the speaker for who he was—an eloquent phony planted by three Southern California educators. The trio had hired an actor and had given him a glowing introduction before his talk.

Most people don't have their guard up when they listen to a speech. They assume what they're hearing is true. And sometimes the most outlandish statements are accepted the most readily without demand for proof. Let a scientist claim that there are exactly 2,564,908 stars in the universe and many are instant believers. Some accept outlandish claims far faster than the more obvious ones. The same listener who accepts at face value the statistics about the number of stars becomes skeptical when he sees a "wet paint" sign outside the auditorium. He's compelled to stick his index finger on the bench to test whether the sign is correct.[1]

So how do we keep from getting conned? How do we make sure we don't use persuasive tactics to con others? Persuasion is powerful because listeners often don't know the tactics used by motivators and don't have guidelines to protect themselves. I would like to suggest three guidelines in applying persuasion: (1) that techniques should be based on truth and reason, (2) that consumers would profit by being less dependent on material possessions and (3) that any use of persuasion should be guided by the law of love found in the Judeo-Christian way of life.

Reason and Truth

It's easy to get taken and few of us can escape the traps set by clever and unscrupulous persuaders. So what can we use as a plumbline to make sure we don't get pulled into accepting a product or idea we'll regret later? For starters, we can be critical listeners and insist on the truth. These twin guidelines are obvious but many have failed to apply them when listening to a sales pitch or considering an idea.

The Sophists of fifth century Athens irked Plato so much because they wanted practical results without concern for truth or reason.[2] If a politician had to lie a little to get elected, so be it, as long as he won. If a used-chariot salesman had to hedge on how many trips the vehicle had taken over the dusty streets of Athens, so what, as long as he could make the sale? The Sophists held that there was no absolute moral law and therefore the rule of the pragmatic should govern human transactions.

The Sophists also taught that emotional appeal got the quickest results. If you could make people feel good, they would probably buy your product or accept your idea. Style, not substance, was their strong suit. In a scathing indictment, Plato declared that persuasion is nothing more than a knack practiced by politicians to gain power and merchants to sell their trinkets. Persuasion would have some merit if virtuous philosophers used it to lead people to the truth and a better life. But in fifth century Athens, persuasion was a way to manipulate others.

Aristotle saw persuasion as morally neutral since it could be applied for good or evil. Aristotle agreed with Plato that a fast-talking charlatan could hoodwink an audience. But he also maintained that rhetoric based on reason and truth could be a valuable tool in trying court cases or leading people to practice virtue. Its *use* made it good or bad. Aristotle's principle of truth and reason is the bedrock of our legal system, philosophic inquiry and the scientific method. If persuaders strive to back claims they make with plenty of supporting evidence, persuasion becomes a powerful instrument of good because it helps achieve justice. In a court case, the insistence on logical argument is the best way judge, jury, prosecutor and defense can arrive at the truth and achieve justice. Cases must be won or lost on evidence and logical validity, not on the mere verbal magic of a talented attorney who knows how to mesmerize a jury. Philosophers and scientists rely on logical argument to validate the claims they make. Conjecture must be verified by hard facts and rigid logic.

But what about other arenas where there is little or no attempt to make sure that reason and truth are the plumblines of persuasion? How can the average consumer protect herself from salespeople who are more interested in making a commission than in giving the customer the best products and service? Or, how can audiences detect the flamboyant orator who hedges on the truth or whose high-charged rhetoric has nothing to do with reason? An effective counter-tactic is critical listening.

Critical Listening

One of Gary Trudeau's most pungent cartoons features a crusty college professor in a turtleneck sweater lecturing to a class on politics. The first frame shows the professor asking students to write an essay on independent thought. The class members scratch down the assignment and everything else the teacher says over the next few minutes. Warming to the occasion, the professor states his opinion that "Jefferson's defense of these basic rights lacked conviction. Okay, any discussion of what I've covered so far? Of course not. You're too busy getting it all down." As the students continue to scribble, the instructor launches into outlandish statements like "The Constitution should never have been ratified. It's a dangerous document. Jefferson was the ANTICHRIST! Democracy is FASCISM! BLACK IS WHITE! NIGHT IS DAY!" After hearing this, one student turns to another and says "Boy, this course is really getting interesting." And his friend replies, "You said it. I didn't know half this stuff." In the final frame, the professor puts his face on the podium and moans "Teaching is dead."

The cartoon, like most good satire, relies on hyperbole. But the truth is many students don't critically examine ideas proposed in class. In the same vein, numerous voters accept at face value whatever a candidate says without testing assertions for logical validity or supporting evidence. Legions of consumers fall for claims made by advertisers who promise much more than they can deliver.

Listeners could better protect themselves by critically testing everything they hear. Any idea or sales pitch should be examined carefully in the light of logical argument and evidence. Do the facts square with the claims being made? Is Bayer a *wonder* drug? Is it really the only pure aspirin on the market? Is Hallmark really the *very best*? Is there enough supporting data to lead to the conclusion the persuader is pitching to the consumer? The habit of critical listening could act as a protective barrier against the siren song of the strong emotional appeal. Listeners can take the stance of a judge and demand that motivators prove their case.

Do we accept ideas on their own merits or believe them because someone we like and respect says they're true? Studies show that most people tend to listen less critically to speakers they perceive as strong or weak on credibility. The eloquent imposter Myron Fox was able to fool a large crowd of well-educated listeners because he enjoyed high credibility through a glowing introduction before the talk. Who would doubt the wise words of an authority on the subject? On the other hand, if an audience perceives a speaker as two quarts low on credibility, they tend to dismiss the ideas because of the speaker and not because the ideas might have merit on their own. While background and expertise should make a difference, the critical listener first examines the validity of the message.

Michael LeBoeuf emphasized that most people accept ideas or buy products with emotion and then justify their decision afterwards with logic.[3] Consumers and voters could avoid regrets later if they would reverse the process. This is no easy job because buying and voting habits have been ingrained over a long time. Placing reason first would help banish disappointment later.

Reason and Ethics

Gordon, the band-leader, is in a bind. He's going to give a speech to potential donors to help collect $5,000 so the high school band can go to Washington D.C. for a national marching competition. This is a worthy cause and he can't let these kids down. He needs a heart-tugging story about a band member who got up every morning at 4 a.m. to deliver papers for two hours to pay his share of the trip. But there's a problem—the band has no such self-sacrificer. So what's the problem with making up a story to add a little spice to the speech and to get more money for something really worthwhile? Some fundraisers, elected officials and salespeople have been fabricating for centuries. What's the harm, especially if the cause is good and no one really gets taken?

Immanuel Kant has provided a useful guideline in deciding whether something is right or wrong. In his "categorical imperative," Kant recommends that when deciding on the ethics of an action—like telling the truth or lying—one should ask if the decision made could be applied to every human being. If I decide to lie, I should imagine the consequences of having everyone else in the world lie also. If we *all* lie, trust would be shattered. Furthermore, by lying, we treat others as objects to be used and not as persons. On a more practical level, if we're caught in a lie, we lose one of the major cornerstones of persuasion—a reputation for integrity.

For the persuader, the "categorical imperative" rule could translate to consistently telling the truth and looking out for the good of the customer. If a salesperson insisted on the truth and backed product claims with solid evidence, two benefits would follow: (1) consumers would be better served and (2) the salesperson would be far more successful over the long haul, because customers buy from people they trust. If a politician tells the unvarnished truth and works for the good of her constituents, she'll stay in office longer because voters want someone they believe in.

Obsessed by Possessions

A second guideline relates to a preoccupation with material goods. Advertisers count on such a preoccupation to market and sell products. Salespeople bank on it to make their commissions. But consumers pay a high price not only in getting strung out on credit but in becoming hooked on the notion that possessions mean happiness. A poster is available in bookstores showing a wealthy man in a fox-hunt outfit, flanked by a Rolls Royce. The caption reads "Poverty sucks." No one will argue with his claim, especially when poverty means going without enough food or decent housing. But the constant striving for wealth has its drawbacks.

There was once a weary traveler who stopped by the country home of a wise man and asked for a night's lodging. The wise man said he would give the traveler two gifts: a place to sleep and some advice on achieving happiness. He then led his guest to the barn and showed him the loft where his mattress for the night would be a bed of hay. Then he said "The second gift I give is to show what you don't need to be happy."

Resisting the siren sound of wealth is tough, especially because the message is pounded home that material possessions bring happiness. Television, movies and magazines overwhelm the senses and numb the brain with this constant theme.

Author Tom Wolfe has coined the term "plutography" and states that plutography is to the 80s what pornography was to the 70s. Publications like *Gentleman's Quarterly* and *Millionaire* have replaced *Playboy* and *Penthouse* as the magazines of choice for those seeking "the" lifestyle. Americans are no longer fascinated by the filthy but by the filthy rich. Millions of us want to know how the wealthy live and how they got that way.

A few years ago *Life* magazine carried two articles. One was about Mother Teresa and the other featured a well-known Hollywood star who was complaining he wasn't finding much happiness in life. Despite money, fame and wealth, he still felt an emptiness in his soul. The two articles stood in stark contrast: Mother Teresa found joy and fulfillment in serving the poor and the Hollywood hero was still looking.

The New Testament contains three times the number of warnings about the danger of riches over the danger of unbridled sexual behavior. Christ states: "Don't store up treasures here on earth where they can erode away or may be stolen. Store them in heaven where they will never lose their value, and are safe from thieves. If your profits are in heaven, your heart will be there too."[4] The pursuit, accumulation and guardianship of wealth can be a full-time job. A few people can own expensive items and not be owned by them, but detachment comes hard for most.

Obviously, there's a big difference between enjoying material objects and being obsessed by them. But for anyone watching television, listening to the radio or reading newspapers and magazines, the message is unrelenting: if you want to be happy, get rich. The combination of skilled advertisers and eager consumers makes the United States one of the world's most fertile grounds for persuasion. Spurred on by the ads, millions spend much of their earnings on items that are thrown away the month payments are finished. What used to be luxuries are now considered necessities.

The advertisers are so good at promoting products that legions of buyers go beyond their budgets as a way of life. Visa, Mastercard and American Express take over where reason and prudence leave off. Millions plunge into bankruptcy because they believe the line that wealth means fulfillment, even if you have to mortgage everything to get it.

Advertisers know well that consumers often don't buy products because they *need* them but because they *want* them. Creating and reinforcing desire is a basic strategy in sales and advertising. Fan the flames of desire and you have a sale. Comedian Flip Wilson used to do a delightful parody of the preacher's wife who came home with two new, expensive dresses and told her husband that "the devil made me do it." She explained to her skeptical mate that she tried to resist at first, but the "devil" kept telling her how good she looked and that she deserved the new clothes. She couldn't make up her mind between the two dresses, so she bought them both.

The Law of Love

A third guideline for applying persuasion is the Judeo-Christian law of love. In a world strewn with examples of persuasion used to inflict harm, this guideline seems the most important. It's a problem to be obsessed by possessions but it's worse to hurt someone and to use persuasion to do the hurting. Let me illustrate this theme with the following true story.

A kindly, middle-aged man sits strapped into a chair. Nearby, a distinguished looking researcher in a white lab coat issues directions to a third person named Bill. The researcher has explained that Bill would be involved in an experiment testing the effects of punishment on learning a set of words. The scientist told Bill to administer an electric shock every time the subject missed an answer. Further, the researcher told him that the level of shock would go up each time the man missed a question. The first shocks would be mild but the voltage would increase to a maximum of 415—a level that would inflict intense pain on the man in the chair.

As the experiment began, the man in the chair started to miss answers. Bill obediently pushed the button to produce a shock. The wrong answers kept coming and Bill continued to push the button. After it became evident that the subject was missing more answers and wanted the experiment to stop, Bill continued anyway, spurred on by the directions of the man in the white lab coat. Even after the subject writhed in pain and shouted that he would no longer participate in the experiment, Bill kept pushing the button.

Such an experiment was conducted by a psychologist named Stanley Milgram at Yale. Unknown to Bill, Milgram was not testing the power of pain on learning, but the impact of authority in motivation. The man strapped in the chair was an actor who pretended to feel the pain. "Bill" was only one of forty subjects who participated in this grizzly exercise.

Over two-thirds of the forty participants followed the lab technician's directions to the end, even though the actor was screaming in pain.

The results of the Milgram experiment were clear. The pain-inflicters were following orders from the leader—no matter how horrifying those orders were. While many of the subjects showed signs of intense anxiety as they continued to push the buttons, they did it anyway.[5] Authority is a powerful persuasive force. The Milgram experiment helps explain the behavior of soldiers during war who blindly follow the orders of their superiors. It also illustrates the power some cult leaders have in persuading their followers not to question the validity of their bizarre doctrines. But persuasion can also be used to show love and kindness.

Jewish author Natalie Goldberg tells about a day she was cleaning out her grandmother's attic. She came across an old oak picture frame with the inscription "Do Your Work As Well As You Can and Be Kind."[6]

Rabbi Harold Kushner reinforces this theme in his book *When All You've Ever Wanted Isn't Enough.*[7] He recalls advice he received from his teacher Abraham Joshua Heschel: "When I was young, I admired clever people. Now I admire kind people."[8] Rabbi Kushner goes on to emphasize two elements that fulfill him: being kind and making something of his life by developing his God-given gifts. The things that really matter in life are not bank accounts or fame but cultivating one's talents and being kind to others.

J. Paul Getty was one of the richest men on earth, but he wasn't one of the happiest. Most of us admire people who have fully utilized their gifts and who have given to others rather than those who have compiled the greatest amount of material wealth. The famous French designer Erte was 95 in December of 1987 and still going strong. Like many other productive artists, he never retired mentally or physically. He said: "If I didn't keep working, I would be bored to death. I work, in general, about five days a week."[9] Two characteristics distinguished Erte. He continues to hone his talents and he's kind. The housekeeper who takes care of him describes him: "He's a wonderful man. To me he is sacred. Every morning he wakes up happy. He laughs and he jokes and he's never angry at anyone."[10]

The hallmark of Christianity is love of neighbor. Christ wanted His disciples to be known by this sign and He demanded that His followers love one another. St. Paul reinforces this key doctrine in his well-known descriptive passage on love. Love is patient and kind, never irritable. If you love someone, you will always believe in him and believe the best. Love is sensitive to the other. And the great paradox is that people who love are also powerful persuaders. Nothing softens someone else more than being the recipient of heart-felt love.

Persuasion aimed at loving one's neighbor yields a double blessing: the recipient gains but so does the giver. The customer gets a quality product at a good price and the salesperson makes a living. The teacher inspires her students to do their best work and, in the process, feels a joy that money could never buy. The nurse coaxes a patient to take the medicine that heals and knows the bone-deep satisfaction that comes from helping others.

The best persuaders are genuinely concerned about their clients or customers. They practice courtroom oratory, preach or sell not merely to help themselves but to benefit others. The teacher who convinces a reluctant student to develop her talents and go on to medical school is doing her a great service. The salesperson who motivates a customer to buy the best quality merchandise at a fair price is doing the consumer a favor. The preacher who persuades a congregation to commit themselves more fully to their spiritual life is engaged in an act of love. The social worker who brings a disillusioned teenager back from the brink of despair and drug addiction is using persuasion as a tool for good. If we really love our neighbor, we want his good. Persuasion becomes a gift to him if what we propose makes him a better person.

There are a lot of shysters trying to hustle everything from snake oil to useless stocks. But the best persuaders put the customer first. Most will believe the phony salesperson once or twice, but after that they won't come back. They won't complain but will find someone who will give them what they want. If we help people get what they want and need—and then some—they are highly open to our persuasive messages. The business owner who goes the extra mile in serving his customer, will not only have a repeat customer but the word will spread that he goes beyond what customers expect. As a result, there is a double blessing for both the persuader and the persuadee. Persuadees are helped to get what they want and persuaders are rewarded for their efforts.

Love and persuasion can be tested by consequences. Christ has said, "By their fruits you shall know them." In applying this principle to motivation, one can ask: do the results of persuasion produce good or bad fruit? Sometimes the standard is easy to apply. Hitler was a charismatic persuader who wielded his power to inflict incredible damage on millions. Jim Jones was so persuasive that he convinced over 600 followers to swallow cianide-laced Kool-aid. On the other hand, Mother Teresa has convinced many to give to the poor. Bob Geldof used his energy and motivational skill to raise enough money to make a dent in the problem of hunger in Africa. Without him, the super-stars he assembled wouldn't have made the hit-record "We Are the World." Mitch Synder used a gritty persistence to get decent housing for the homeless in Washington, D.C. In these cases, persuasion became a tool to benefit thousands who couldn't help themselves.

If we really have in mind the best interest of the other, persuasion is an instrument of good. We can be mistaken about what is good for the other person, be it an idea or a product, but most of the time the rule of the "good of others" applies rather easily. Do our persuasive efforts make people better or worse? Do we help or hurt those we persuade? Are we helped or hurt by someone else's efforts to motivate us? The answers to these questions provide reliable guidelines.

A few years ago, Jack Lemon starred in a movie called *Mass Appeal*. The film featured Lemon as a slightly neurotic but loveable priest who was supervising an idealistic and spirited seminarian. In one of the most poignant lines in the movie, the young man said he had discovered the secret of happiness after a long search. Happiness was not to be found in material possessions but in quietly serving other people. Deep joy usually comes as a by-product of serving others. Persuasion is one way to serve.

In this book, I've tried to explain how persuasion works, how we can use it when we want to persuade others and how we can protect ourselves from getting manipulated. Some of the people in these pages were noble, some were rogues and others were a mixture of virtues and faults. Many, but not all, were Catholic. There has been no attempt to defend the unattractive features of famous persuaders like Urban II or John Kennedy. Urban's eleventh century crusade speech may have been one of the most powerful in history, but it was basically a call to violence. John Kennedy led Americans on a much needed journey through Camelot, but he had his personal flaws, which, had they been known at the time, would have eroded his persuasive effectiveness.

I've identified most strongly with the Aristotelian perspective that persuasion is neither good nor bad in itself, but becomes so through its use by people. Those who have applied this art form out of love and a concern for others reflect the power of persuasion for good. Those who have misused it to make a quick, dishonest buck or to prop up their twisted egos and keep their followers in line demonstrate its power to hurt.

Persuasion is indispensable in a democratic society. It drives our political machines, helps achieve justice and keeps the economy going. Persuasion can lift up or tear down, inspire or seduce, build or destroy. The choice of how to use its power is an important one.

Summary of Key Points

1. It's easy to get conned. The brightest and best educated listeners can occasionally get taken in by smooth-talking persuaders. Therefore, it helps to have guidelines for persuasion.

2. For both persuaders and targets of persuasive messages, one such guideline is truth and reason. The motivator who tells the truth is far more effective because listeners hate the lie and will show their displeasure by voting for someone else or taking their business to another store. Reason provides a solid barometer for testing persuasion. Logical argument is not as certain as mathematics but it gives us a chance to get as close as possible. Insistence on ample evidence and avoidance of logical fallacies can help weed out the effective but illogical pitch based on emotion.

3. While advertising and sales stimulate the economy, they've also helped create an obsession with material goods. Consumers can monitor whether the appealing ad is promoting products that help fulfill human needs or is making luxuries seem like necessities.

4. A third guideline is the law of love based on the Judeo-Christian perspective. If persuasion hurts, robs or degrades, it shouldn't be used. If persuaders are interested primarily in the good of the customer, voter or friend, then the art of motivation is a blessing.

Chapter Notes

Chapter 1

1. Joseph R. Strayer and Dana C. Munro, *The Middle Ages: 395-1500* (New York: Appleton-Century Crofts, 1970), p. 228.

2. *Ibid.*

3. Leon Festinger was one of the first to identify the uneasiness felt by persuadees. For a fuller explanation of "cognitive dissonance," please see Charles Larson, *Persuasion: Reception and Responsibility,* 4th ed. (Belmont, California: Wadsworth, 1986), pp. 42-45.

4. *How to Get People to Do Things* (New York: Ballantine Books), 1979, p. 3.

5. For a more complete explanation of how attitudes work in persuasion, please see Victoria O'Donnell and June Kable, *Persuasion: An Interactive Dependency Approach* (New York: Random House, 1982), p. 35.

6. *Ibid.*

Chapter 2

1. *Influence: the New Psychology of Modern Persuasion* (New York, William Morrow, 1984), p. 163.

2. Book I, Ch. 2 of *The Rhetoric.*

3. See John T. Molloy, *The New Dress for Success* (New York: Warner Books, Inc., 1988).

4. For a more complete description of the debate, please refer to Theodore White, *The Making of the President, 1960* (New York: Atheneum, 1961), pp. 279-295.

5. Book I, Ch. 2 of *The Rhetoric*.

6. Donald Joy, *Rebonding: Preventing and Restoring Damaged Relationships,* (Waco, Texas: Word Books, 1986), p. 107.

7. Molloy, *op. cit.*

8. (New York: Simon and Schuster, 1977), p. 121.

9. (New York: Dell, 1972).

10. *TV Guide*, January 10, 1987, p. 27.

11. (New York: Random House, 1970), p. 203.

12. "Charisma's Not Just for Pols and Preachers," article by Margot Gibb-Clark, *Spokesman-Review Chronicle,* December 20, 1987, pp. 1-2.

Chapter 3

1. See Sharon Begley, John Carey and Ray Sawhill, *Newsweek,* February 7, 1983 for a fuller explanation of where emotions reside in the brain.

2. Adolph Hitler, *Mein Kampf,* trans. by Ralph Manheim (Boston: Houghton Mifflin, 1973), p. 469.

3. Movie, *Minister of Hate,* produced by CBS and narrated by Walter Cronkite.

4. *The Complete Works of Shakespeare,* ed. Hardin Craig (Chicago: Scott, Foresman and Co., 1961), p. 786.

5. Howard Bremer, *Richard M. Nixon 1913-   : Chronology-Documents-Bibliography Aids* (New York: Dobbs Ferry, 1975), p. 90.

6. See *Influence*, p. 29.

Chapter 4

1. Coe was tried twice. Chief County Prosecutor Donald Brockett worked the first trial with Patricia Thompson. After the conviction, Coe's mother Ruth was arrested for trying to pay an assassin to maim Brockett and Judge George Shields. The "hit man" was an undercover police officer. Coe was later given a new trial because the Washington State Supreme Court ruled that the first trial contained errors of evidence. In the second trial, Patricia Thompson was a co-prosecutor with Stephen Matthews.

2. Chris Peck article, *Spokesman-Review*, August 2, 1981, p. A12.

3. Fred Coe later changed his name to "Kevin."

4. For an excellent description of the concept "guilty beyond a reasonable doubt," please see Vincent Bugliosi *Until Death Do Us Part* (New York: Bantam Books, 1979), p. 339.

5. Quotation taken from Chris Peck's article, *Spokesman Review*, August 2, 1981, p. A12.

6. In January, 1988, a divided Washington State Supreme Court threw out three of the four convictions on the grounds that hypnotized victims could not testify. That left only one conviction intact and made Coe eligible for parole within four years.

7. *Persuasion: Understanding, Practice and Analysis* (Menlo Park, California: Addison Wesley, 1976), p. 198.

8. *American Orators of the 20th Century: Critical Studies and Sources,* Bernard Duffy and Halford Ryan, ed. (New York: Greenwood Press, 1987).

9. Halford Ross Ryan, *American Rhetoric from Roosevelt to Reagan* (Prospect Heights, Illinois: Waveland Press Inc., 1987), p. 152.

10. *Ibid.*, p. 153.

11. *Ibid.*, p. 154.

12. *Ibid.*

13. *Getting to Yes* (Harrisonburg, Virginia: R.R. Donnelley and Sons Co., 1981).

Chapter 5

1. Joy, *Rebonding*.

2. *The New Celibacy: Why More Men and Women are Abstaining from Sex—and Enjoying It* (New York: McGraw-Hill, 1980), p. 100.

3. *Ibid.*, p. 122.

4. *Treasury of Humor* (Boston: Houghton Mifflin, 1971).

5. Romans 7:15. Translation from the *Living Bible*.

6. *Spokesman Review*, Sept. 28, 1987, p. A10.

7. King James version.

8. *Lives of Saints with Excerpts from Their Writings*, ed. Joseph Vann (New York: John Crawley and Co. Inc., 1954), pp. 300-303.

Chapter 6

1. See Vance Packard, *The Hidden Persuaders*, Chap. 15 "The Psycho-Seduction of Children" (New York: David McKay Co., 1957), pp. 157-166.

2. See Stephen Fox, *The Mirror Makers: a History of American Advertising and Its Creators* (New York: William Morrow and Co., 1984), pp. 183-184.

3. *Ibid.*, p. 223.

4. ABC News, morning program for November 18, 1987.

5. See *How to Sell Anything to Anybody* (New York: Simon and Schuster, 1977), p. 120.

Chapter 7

1. Article from *Spokesman-Review*, August 10, 1987, p. 6.

2. Article from *Spokesman-Review*, February 29, 1984, p. 13. The National Cult Awareness Network of Chicago also provides a list of those cults considered destructive.

3. *Persuasion: Understanding, Practice and Analysis* (Menlo Park, California: Addison Wesley, 1976), pp. 94-96.

4. *Newsweek*, p. 74.

5. Christopher Edwards, *Crazy for God: the Nightmare of Cult Life* (Englewood Cliffs, New Jersey: Prentice-Hall, 1979), pp. 10-11.

6. *Newsweek*, December 4, 1976, p. 72.

7. For a more complete explanation of brainwashing, please see J.A.C. Brown, *Techniques of Persuasion: From Propaganda to Brainwashing* (Baltimore, Maryland: Penguin Books, 1972), pp. 267-293.

8. For a detailed treatment of Bailey's "brainwashing" defense, see Shana Alexander, *Anyone's Daughter: the Times and Trials of Patty Hearst* (New York: Viking Press, 1979), pp. 46-48.

9. See *The Chronicle of Higher Education*, March 9, 1983, p. 7.

10. See Kenneth Burke, "The Rhetoric of Hitler's 'Battle'" in *The Philosophy of Literacy Form* (Baton Rouge: Louisana State University Press, 1967).

Chapter 8

1. O'Donnell and Kable, *op. cit.*, p. 194.

2. For more information on McLuhan's theories, please refer to his two works, *The Gutenberg Galaxy* (Toronto: the University of Toronto Press, 1962) and *Understanding Media* (New York: McGraw-Hill, 1964).

3. *TV Guide,* November 28, 1987, pp. 5-6.

4. *Spokesman-Review,* January 18, 1988, p. A7.

5. "Intervening Variables in the TV Violence-Aggression Relation: Evidence from Two Countries," in *Developmental Psychology,* September 1984, pp. 746-775.

6. Facts taken from an article by Bernard Coughlin, S.J., "Preferences or Principles," *Inland Register,* March 3, 1988, p. 9.

7. Material from article by Jennifer Lowe in Los Angeles, California, *Daily News,* reported in *Spokesman-Review,* February 3, 1988, p. C1.

8. *Ibid.*

9. Matthew 6:19-21, 24, *Living Bible* translation.

10. For an explanation of neurolinguistic programming, please refer to Richard Bandler and John Grinder, *Frogs into Princes* (Moab, Utah: Real People Press, 1979).

11. (New York: Simon and Schuster, 1987), p. 62.

12. For a fuller explanation of Rank's model, please see Larson, *op. cit.*, pp. 13-20.

Chapter 9

1. Dan Nimmo, *The Political Persuaders: The Techniques of Modern Election Campaigns* (Englewood Cliffs, New Jersey: 1970), pp. 29-30.

2. Rebecca Nappi, *Spokesman-Review,* March 24, 1988, p. C1.

3. *Ibid.*

4. Please see Erwin Bettinghaus, *Persuasive Communication* (New York: Holt, Rinehart and Winston, 1968), pp. 185-188.

5. *How To Win Customers and Keep Them for Life* (New York: G. P. Putnam's Sons, 1987), p. 40.

6. Teri Kwal Gamble and Michael Gamble, *Communication Works,* 2nd ed. (New York: Random House, 1987), pp. 348.

7. John Salisbury, director of news and special projects at radio station KXL, Portland, Oregon.

Chapter 10

1. Idea taken from a speech by Carolyn Warner, Phoenix, Arizona, 1973.

2. See Plato's *Gorgias.*

3. LeBoeuf, *op. cit.,* p. 39.

4. Matthew 6: 19-21, *Living Bible* translation.

5. Cialdini, *op. cit.,* pp. 203-214.

6. *Writing Down the Bones* (Boston: Shambhala, 1986), p. XI.

7. *When All You've Ever Wanted Isn't Enough: The Search for a Life that Matters* (New York: Pocket Books, 1987).

8. *Ibid.,* p. 58.

9. Story by Robin Abcarian in The *Spokesman-Review Chronicle,* December 12, 1987, p. C4.

10. *Ibid.*